ENDORSI

"It's with blurry eyes and a soft heart I implore you to take this book ... ... wide to the One who searches our innermost being, and believe you will be transformed in the next 40 days. There are many books and devotionals promising such, and I love many of them. However, there is something unique about Julie's writings, and there's no fresh way to communicate the difference except that it is anointed, and it is for now. Set your quest for more Bible knowledge aside to seek Jesus (John 5:39) and how you can posture your heart to partner with Him in this unprecedented time in history. You were meant to be a revivalist."

Heather Senter, 70 Women in 70 Cities: Georgia

"Two of God's promises are, *'Draw near to God and He will draw near to you (James 4:8, NASB)'* and *'"You will seek Me and find Me when you search for Me with all your heart (Jeremiah 29:13, NASB).'"* This author regularly does this, and as a result, she finds God, and He is able to speak to her His love, His vision for His creation, His wisdom, and His plans. Not only does Julie share what she receives, but she gives the reader a hunger for and ability to enjoy God's presence for herself. In this book of devotions, Julie passionately and winsomely conveys God's truth and timely counsel to His precious daughters to help them discern what God is doing today. A must read."

Patti Evans, 70 Women in 70 Cities: South Carolina

"This book left me inspired, challenged, excited, and most of all awestruck at the powerful love of Jesus. I could hear the drumbeat of revival as I read Julie's words. She has captured a vision for the redemptive love of Christ to wash over this country and the world in a new and powerful way. I truly believe Julie has been led by the Holy Spirit to raise this battle cry, and, after reading her soul's words, I don't want to miss the battle. Julie has a gift for powerfully moving hearts into action. However, she does this with a grace and gentleness, causing people to take heed and answer the call to go."

Peggy Ike, 70 Women in 70 Cities: Washington

"Whether in the pages of her writing or sitting across a table over a cup of coffee, Julie is what one might call a 'super spreader.' With a sense of urgency, she beckons each of us to a greater intimacy with our Bridegroom, fully engaging us in worshipping, listening, digging, pondering, and responding. Julie's heart, reflected through her words, compels us to arise and press forward for eternal impact in our cities and around the world. It is not uncommon for women to tell me, 'I have never heard this language before,' and then continue to speak of how God is drawing them back to His heart and path for holiness. Julie's life and words speak boldly to the hearts of women to not merely survive this world but to thrive in their calling as they grasp the vision God has for each of us."

Ali Despres, Arise Regional Director, East-West

"If you desire a deeper intimate walk with the Lord, then this devotional is for you! September 2020, I was introduced to Julie King's first devotional book, 'Arise My Darling.' The book was so impactful that it took my spiritual walk of four decades to a whole new level. Many years ago a very wise Christian counselor told me that one can only teach and help people as far as one's spiritual journey has taken them. Julie King's love and passion for God comes from a place of deep wisdom and maturity! I am confident Julie's new devotional 'Revivalist Arise' will ignite your spirit and open your heart to fall deeper in love with our Lord Jesus Christ."

Nannette Aviles Simpson, The Wellness Coach,
70 Women in 70 Cities: California

"Julie King has surrendered her life to Jesus in exchange for what God desires to do through her. Already, she is leading hundreds of women (and men) to reconsider God's radical call on their lives. Her message to an anxious and angry world screaming the virtue of self-worship is to gently point us back to our Creator. She reminds us of God's kindness. She exhorts us to consider the lateness of the hour. She compels us to die to our flesh in order that the Holy Spirit can work fully in us. Revivalist points us to the only One who can bring peace and healing to our broken hearts with a call to action to evangelize while it is still called today. '"See, I am doing a new thing! Now it springs up; do you not perceive it? I am making a way in the wilderness and streams in the wasteland (Isaiah 43:19).'"*

Kristin Hill, APRN MSN RNFA FNP-C,
70 Women in 70 Cities: Texas

"In her book, 'Revivalist Arise,' Julie again brings treasures with each daily devotion. From the worship song selections, which usher in the sweetness of God's presence, to her stories and prayers filled with Scripture and truth, her words encourage and convict the reader to know Jesus more intimately. She challenges us to trust and to step up and embrace our calling to be strong and not afraid! Her writing is vulnerable and tender yet strong and intentional with what she needs and knows Jesus will do for His children. I encourage you, read these devotionals out loud for a stronger sense of God's power through them. Then command God's army of angels to take flight with this Word He has released and cover the globe. I am most grateful Julie King is my sister in Christ."

Kathy Garrett, The Charis Group

REVIVALIST ARISE

Encounters with Jesus that Position You to Carry the Fires of Revival

JULIE KING

A 40-DAY DEVOTIONAL JOURNEY

Revivalist Arise
Encounters with Jesus that Position You to Carry the Fires of Revival

Julie King | East-West Publishing

To contact the author: jking@eastwest.org

For updated information on events, trips, resources, and ways to get involved, visit our website at www.eastwest.org/arise.

ISBN (Print): 978-1-7374997-0-1
ISBN (E-book): 978-1-7374997-2-5
East-West Publishing
Plano, TX

Other books by Julie King:
Arise My Darling: Encounters with Jesus to Ignite Passion, Worship, and Wonder.
Published by East-West Publishing, 2020.

DEDICATION

I dedicate this book to my warrior sister, Alexandria Watkins. Your armor is dented and scratched, and your feet are ablaze with the fire of God. You have been on the battlefield since March of 2020, tirelessly saving as many as you could. It's been an honor to stand with you, shoulder to shoulder, at the feet of Jesus as He gets you ready to bring forth His purposes on the Earth in even greater measure and increase. I honor you, Alexandria, and count it a joy to run hard after Jesus with you. Thank you for your life of courage, passion, sacrifice, and surrender. You are deeply loved.

SPECIAL THANKS

To my beloved husband and four daughters, I love you and I pray my life brings you praise at the city gates. Projects like this see the finish line because I have five of you standing with me. Your wisdom, love, and encouragement enable me to soar.

Thank you to my donors who said, "Yes," to running with me personally as I launched out this year. Your faith has anchored me. Thank you for sowing into God's calling on my life. I pray every ounce of harvest that comes forth from this book and my life bears abundant fruit in your lives.

To my fiery and faith-filled team God is raising up to build and expand Arise, we are doing this together, and I am so inspired, encouraged, and thankful for you. Let's go find as many women as we can, get their lamps filled with oil, and have them running into this harvest field. Thanks for saying, "yes," and for stepping into this important hour.

Mary Ethel Eckard, Caleb Read, Lindsey M., Mitch Little, and Greg Despres, thank you for bringing this book to life. I am so grateful for this gracious publishing, marketing, and editing team.

Kristen Shuler, I love you and honor you. Thank you for leading me so well and for being a woman of fearless courage. The favor of God is on you and it is glorious to behold.

And at the very foundation of my life are two people who gave me the roadmap of faith—to follow Jesus into every unknown no matter the cost. Mom and Dad, I honor you all my days.

FOREWORD

You can feel it all around and within you. Now is the beginning of the greatest outpouring of the Spirit of Grace this world has ever known. And it is only going to become greater in scope and larger in mass. Within the heart of countless men and women, boys and girls, the Holy Spirit is whispering to some and shouting to others:

> I am here and ready to take over this generation. Will you
> join Me?

Not many devotionals prepare you to answer, "Yes," to this question. This new 40-day devotional by Julie King was penned for this purpose. She has a unique way of writing that allows the reader to seamlessly step into the room where she is standing with Christ. In this sanctified place, you tangibly feel the heartbeat of Christ, His unwavering passion and unstoppable zeal. It is here you experience the Living Word made flesh, who dwells among us. Few writers have the distinct ability to walk you into this holy place. Julie King is one of them.

I met this wide-eyed, beautiful, and zealous sister when she walked into the home where I was speaking. I immediately knew there was something special about her, and I needed to know her more. She was confident but not proud. She carried a quiet demeanor; but when she spoke, she was sure and certain, sharp, and tuned into the Lord. She had an uncommon focus and intention that exuded confident assurance that she would not be swayed off the Lord's vision for her life. I wanted to know more about that vision. Over time we were able to break bread, laugh, talk, and pray.

During these times, I got to know the heart of this most excellent saint, one who brings a wellspring of the knowledge of the resurrected and exalted Christ and His passion for souls everywhere she goes.

Because I believe food at a restaurant is better when you know the chef and books are more appealing to read when you have heard the author speak, I want to introduce you to this passionate woman after the heart of God, Julie King.

Honestly, I could sit and listen to Julie talk for hours. She is a child of missionary parents. She tells of her parents imploring God to send them to the most "dangerous places in the world." God answered and did just that. This is the uncommon faith seed from which Julie was born. Like her parents, her passion and pursuit are for the exalted Christ to be made known to the nations. "Lord send me. I want to take Jesus to the world" is her cry. The Lord has answered her cry and has called and anointed her for this great task.

Over the years, Julie has taken the gospel of Christ to the ends of the Earth and to the top of some exceptionally large mountains. She and her teams have traversed mountains in Africa and South Asia to bring the saving message of Christ to the remotest villages on the planet. She is extreme for Jesus, and it emanates through the pages of this devotional.

Most recently she is fulfilling the vision the Lord gave her of equipping and empowering women to arise and step into one of their God given purposes—sharing the gospel message in their communities and cities. To this end, Julie has set her sights on 70 cities based on Numbers 11:16-17. In addition to this national Arise movement, she continues to take teams of women to unreached areas of the world.

Honestly, when I consider Julie's dedication to Christ and His calling on her life, I am more enthralled at her new devotional. The Scripture says,

"Let another man praise you, and not your own mouth ... (Proverbs 27:2a, NKJV)." I praise Julie King. This faithful sister is worthy of honor and praise. Her dedication to fan the flames of revival oozes from her heart and from these pages. You cannot read phrases like "let's go make history with God" and not want the flames of revival fire in your own life.

This devotional helps to center and direct your heart to what God has called you to do in this last hour. You will leave each reading hungry and provoked to ask the Lord for more of Him. No doubt, this hunger will be satisfied as God begins to pour His Spirit into your life and revive any parched or dry places. I encourage you to receive this devotional and the next 40 days as a gift from our Father, personally to you. As you read, envision yourself receiving a taste of the most wonderful, life-giving delicacies from the Lord. Know that as you dine on Him and consume His words of life, He is equipping you to partner with Him to carry His holy flame. What an honor to be considered for this highly valued and worthy task.

All those who choose this 40-day journey of encounters with Jesus will find a new river of life flowing into their heart. This river will renew their passion for the resurrected Christ, restore the joy of their salvation, and prepare the heart for bold faith: the asking of the Lord to *"make the nations your inheritance, the ends of the earth your possession (Psalm 2:8)."*

I love receiving arrows from the Lord. Arrows help us win the battle. This devotional is a now arrow in the Lord's quiver, an arrow He has made ready and sent to our generation to help us run our race of faith and finish it well. Our race of faith is not common with any prior generation. Yes, there have been great revivals, but none like that which is purposed in the heart of our Father. I don't know about you, but I signed up to partner with the Holy Spirit in this great move of God. Through this 40-day devotional, the Lord has provided the arrows, and Julie has stirred the flame, both to equip and ready us for this hour. I challenge you to take the arrows and the flame and use them to allow the Holy Spirit to set your heart ablaze. I guarantee you, I will.

I am so grateful to be alive and to be counted worthy to know Christ. I know you feel the same. Let's do this together. Let's show Jesus our love toward Him. If we have never given Christ our all, let's do it now. This is our moment; this is our hour. Let the Lord have His way in you. This is one decision I guarantee you will never regret, not ever.

I so look forward to seeing you at the finish line. Until then, keep your eyes on Jesus, the only One worthy of our devotion and praise.

In Christ and in His love,

Christina L. McCracken-Nussle, J.D.
Lawyer and Advocate for Christ
www.bomglaw.com
www.counselor-to-counselor.com

Author of the books: "Divine Restoration, from COUNSELOR to Counselor (and Workbook)," and "Live for That Day, Garnering Rewards at the Judgment Seat of Christ"

CONTENTS

INTRODUCTION
AWAKE, ARISE, AND COME ALIVE

Daughters of the Most High God, there's an invitation
resounding from the throne room of Heaven:

Awake, arise, and come fully alive!

Can you hear the roar of Jesus for His Bride? He is inviting us to come
fully alive in Him—every part of who we are.

As I sat with the Lord in preparation for this 40-day journey, I could feel
the excitement of Heaven on our passionate pursuit of Jesus. The eyes of
the Lord have roamed the Earth and found hundreds and hundreds of
His daughters positioned in longing, surrender, and love for the One their
hearts adore. So here we sit and commune and wait and listen and adore.

*"I promise that I will never leave you helpless or abandon you as
orphans—I will come back to you! Soon I will leave this world and they
will see me no longer, but you will see me, because I will live again, and
you will come alive too. So when that day comes, you will know that I
am living in the Father and that you are one with me, for I will be living
in you. Those who truly love me are those who obey my commands."*
-John 14:18-21a, TPT

Looking at the passage above, Jesus was ready to leave His people, the
ones He manifested the kingdom of Heaven to, over and over. The cross
before Him would be to secure their adoption as sons and daughters. He

promised, *"I will come back to you (John 14:18, TPT)!"* He was going to give them the promised Holy Spirit—their *parákletos,* who is our defense attorney, counselor, comforter, advocate, encourager, one who is called to help us. Jesus knew we couldn't fully come alive unless He gave His life on the cross and deposited Himself in us by His Spirit. Only then, in the finished work of the cross, would we come alive in every sense of reality—spiritually, physically, emotionally, etc. Seal this reality with His blood and the promised Holy Spirit and off we run in freedom, victory, hope, and glory.

*"Whoever passionately loves me will be passionately loved by my Father.
And I will passionately love him in return and will reveal myself to him."*
-John 14:21b, TPT

Do you know there's nothing you can do to make our Father love you more or love you less? You are securely and undoubtedly loved, no matter what. But what you do with that passionate love makes all the difference in the world—literally. He will manifest His life and His passionate love for the world through your surrender. That's what this 40-day journey is about—positioning your heart to be transformed by His passionate love for you and for the world He died for.

It's time to awaken to that love. It's time to view disappointment, chaos, hurt, pain, and even great joy through that lens. It's time to place your heart on the operating table of Heaven and ask God to do heart surgery—to clean out, realign, reconnect, heal, shock your heart back to life (for those who have been in a spiritual wilderness), and unclog. Oh, that passion would flow through your heart. Oh, that the blood of Jesus—that is your victory, healing, freedom, and life—would pulse through your spiritual veins.

Revival isn't just for the lost, dear sister.
Revival is for the people of God to come alive again.

I invite you to position your heart before the Lord and converse with Him over two things. Then journal how He responds to you.

- Search me, oh God, and reveal to me anything that is holding my heart back from complete passion for You as we prepare for these 40 days together.
- What do You want to say to me today as it pertains to Your passionate love for me? What is Your desire for my heart and life?

There is a great call to intercession for the Body of Christ. God must grant people the genuine faith and the fervent desire for prayer. But every revival in history was birthed on the foundation of prayer, and now it's your turn.

Are you ready to launch into this journey of
intimacy and encounter? Jesus is ready.
It's going to be glorious.

Lord, thank You for what You have orchestrated because of Your marvelous love for me. I wait in expectation and surrender. I pray for an anointing over my ears and mind that I hear the words You speak every day. Open my ears and my understanding to discern Your voice and receive Your words of life. May I will come awake and arise to new life. May the old wilderness places be gone, and new encounters come. Take me on the mountain with You for 40 days and pour out Your wisdom and revelation. Let me be ignited with the fire of Your presence and overflow with the joy of my salvation. Speak to me about the depth of Your love for me and for those who don't yet know You. It is time to passionately love You with all that I am, nothing withheld, and to passionately love the lost who need to know You, Jesus. Lord, will You put my lamp in Your hands and fill it to overflowing with Your oil? Prepare me for Your coming, and prepare Your glorious Bride. I worship You and thank You for Your goodness and passionate love. In the wondrous name of Jesus, amen.

"Let us rejoice and be glad and give him glory!
For the wedding of the Lamb has come, and
his bride has made herself ready."
-Revelation 19:7

Listen to this worship song: "Come Alive" by Dante Bowe

Day One

---✦---

THE STAGE IS SET

I am wide-eyed with expectation. Our Father doesn't withhold His heart or Himself. He desires us to be prepared, alert, and ready with our lamps filled with oil. The Holy Spirit is the Great Revealer of mysteries and hidden things—our Great Counselor. And right now, He is bringing forth hidden things with accelerated revelation and understanding (John 16:12-15).

> *"'Just as it was in the days of Noah, so also will it be in the days of the Son of Man. People were eating, drinking, marrying and being given in marriage up to the day Noah entered the ark. Then the flood came and destroyed them all.*
>
> *"'It was the same in the days of Lot. People were eating and drinking, buying and selling, planting and building. But the day Lot left Sodom, fire and sulfur rained down from heaven and destroyed them all.*
>
> *"'It will be just like this on the day the Son of Man is revealed. On that day no one who is on the housetop, with possessions inside, should go down to get them. Likewise, no one in the field should go back for anything. Remember Lot's wife! Whoever tries to keep their life will lose it, and whoever loses their life will preserve it. I tell you, on that night two people will be in one bed; one will be taken and the other left. Two women will be grinding grain together; one will be taken and the other left.'*

"'Where, Lord?' they asked.

"He replied, 'Where there is a dead body, there the vultures will gather.'"
-Luke 17:26-37

As the Lord placed Luke 17 on my heart two days in a row, I went on a treasure hunt to find out what He was saying. When I got to the above verses, they jumped off the page. There was a word of urgency from the Holy Spirit even as I prayed for what to write. Urgency is defined as importance requiring swift action; a force or impulse that impels or constrains. Urgency will impact how we live out the Word of God we read and follow.

Can you imagine what that day will be like for the one who remains? Those of us who know Jesus will be taken with Him, but according to this passage, there will be those who have been in intimate relationship with us who will not know where we have gone. They will search and search, and I believe there will be many grieving and distraught people left hopeless and in despair.

But that day has not come yet. Although we live in the ellipsis of the last words of Jesus in Revelation 22:20, *"Yes, I am coming soon,"* He has still given us time. Time is our greatest weapon and tool and gift right now. (That's why busyness is the greatest tool of the enemy.) The Lord gave us a time of divine reset in the 2020 quarantine season to get on His kingdom agenda and to return to Him. But we must heed these passages of Scripture with urgency and sobriety. Jesus is returning for His Bride. But His great love for the world keeps Him from coming because He doesn't want anyone to miss this.

"And this gospel of the kingdom will be preached in the whole world
as a testimony to all nations, and then the end will come."
-Matthew 24:14

I was sitting with the Lord one morning and penned these words:

I am drawing a line in the sand, and it will become more and more clear—those who are with Me and those who are against Me. I will reveal the inner parts of each person's heart, and the defining line will become even more clear.

You will see those bent on My agenda and those bent on their own agenda. I have desired to use this time of **reset** not to start over and do the same things as before, but to begin in a new way; the old way is gone.

Reset for a different road—a different trajectory—the right path of righteousness. Many will change habits, activities, pursuits, desires. Some will go their own way, back to what they originally desired and pursued because that was a comfort to them. They are unable to leave the world behind for the new thing.

You will see some who never knew Me (although they thought they had). I must awaken them to truth in this hour. There will be a great repentance. People will long for Me because I will make it clearly evident that I am the only One who satisfies. If people will allow Me, I will even change the things their hearts crave.

When I say I am doing a new thing, you better believe it is true. I am making new pathways in the desert. I am opening new doors of expedition and exploration into who I am. I am opening wide the door of invitation across the Earth and revealing My love in the most tangible ways. It will not be hard to find Me. I am making Myself known among the nations in rapid acceleration.

Then the Holy Spirit took me to this Scripture:

"For the earth will be filled with the knowledge of the glory of Lord as the waters cover the sea."
-Habakkuk 2:14

I am covering the Earth with My presence to know that I am God. I will be exalted in the nations. I will be exalted in this nation. Those who oppose Me or oppose My righteousness, I will oppose. I will eliminate their influence and take away their authority. They will be like Nebuchadnezzar, who was reduced to nothing. The wicked will be pushed back in this hour so that righteousness may cover the Earth, and all men's deeds will be seen for what they are. I am releasing a fear of the Lord that will leave those whose hearts are for Me in awe and wonder. The wicked will be silenced. Truth will prevail and be unearthed. People will see evil for what it truly is.

Beloved, I share this because there is a weightiness in my heart, and I implore you to live for that day. Live for the day when you will be united with your glorious Bridegroom. Throw off everything that entangles you and run with passion to the one Lover of your soul. Live with your passions and affections not for the world, but for Him. Live so your life proclaims, like Paul, *"For to me, to live is Christ ... (Philippians 1:21)."* Take hold of the urgency the Holy Spirit will give if you just ask Him for it.

"I never lay my head on the pillow without thinking that perhaps before I awake, the final morning may have dawned. I never begin my work without thinking that He may interrupt it to begin His own. And every night before we go to sleep, we ought to say, 'He may come tonight.' Every day when we get out our tools and go to work, 'This may be the last day's work I'll do.'" -G. Campbell Morgan

Holy Spirit, speak to the deepest recesses of my heart. Jesus, speak with a resounding invitation to come to You, to lay everything my heart desires before You, to trade my desires for Your desires. Sanctify me through and through to carry the fire of Heaven deep within my bones, as described by Jeremiah—a fire he could not contain. Let me be marked by passion, zeal, and urgency. Anoint me to live for that day—the coming of Jesus for His Bride. Lord, enable me to speak Your word with boldness and courage, that none I love would live eternity apart from You. And Father, pour out Your love on me; let it crash over me and leave me undone. Awaken and refresh me, in Jesus' name.

Listen to this worship song: "Father" by VoxMusic

HE'S SAVED THE BEST TILL NOW

*"On the third day a wedding took place at Cana in Galilee.
Jesus' mother was there, and Jesus and his disciples had also
been invited to the wedding. When the wine was gone,
Jesus' mother said to him, 'They have no more wine.'*

*"'Woman, why do you involve me?' Jesus replied. 'My hour has not yet come.'
"His mother said to the servants, 'Do whatever he tells you.'*

*"Nearby stood six stone water jars, the kind used by the Jews for
ceremonial washing, each holding from twenty to thirty gallons.*

*"Jesus said to the servants, 'Fill the jars with
water'; so they filled them to the brim.*

*"Then he told them, 'Now draw some out and
take it to the master of the banquet.'*

*"They did so, and the master of the banquet tasted the water that
had been turned into wine. He did not realize where it had come
from, though the servants who had drawn the water knew. Then
he called the bridegroom aside and said, 'Everyone brings out the*

choice wine first and then the cheaper wine after the guests have
had too much to drink; but you have saved the best till now.'"
-John 2:1-10

In the above passage, Jesus stands at a pivotal crossover between his private and public ministry. This moment changed everything personally for Jesus. What was hidden would now be revealed. The Son of God was stepping onto the scene in a new way with signs and wonders. A historical shift was taking place.

Before Jesus were six empty water jugs. In Scripture, the number six is the number for man. I wonder if those six pots represent six disciples who were following Jesus at that point. Nonetheless, we have a number that is symbolic of man. Ordinary water pots were then filled with choice wine. This place of celebration launches Jesus' public ministry.

In this hour we are being awakened to the truest gospel—the power, signs, wonders, miracles, and reality of the cross and resurrection—for the love of the world Jesus died for. He wants to take the wine of our lives and the things that have felt crushing and bring forth something so beautifully intoxicating. We are coming out of hiding and hibernation, sleep and slumber, and awakening to what He has prepared us to carry. Your life can be filled to the brim, and the overflow can literally change everything for those who simply take a sip.

Six stone jars meant for cleansing were turned into pots of celebration and wonder at this wedding in Cana. What if someone took a drink of your life—would they taste the miracle of new wine?

This is a now word for us that hangs in my spirit. I believe the best has been saved till now. This generation has been made ready to move in exploits that are greater than any generation preceding them. In the pressing of this time, He is making new wine. And He is preparing us to carry it in this new era.

The new wine needs new wineskins that have been prepared and made ready. After Pentecost, the onlookers looked at the disciples who were so full of the Spirit that many thought they had too much wine when indeed their lives were simply in overflow.

We have an invitation to be filled to the brim with new wine for this new era. I believe He's saved the best wine till now. More than 3 billion people have yet to taste it. It's time to let the overflow come.

One night, I ordered takeout for my family. As the delivery driver handed me the order, he said, "God bless you. Jesus loves you. Don't be sad because Jesus loves you." I was overcome because the overflow from the delivery man touched my life. I had been overwhelmed with a weightiness that came out of nowhere. The Holy Spirit sent that man to remind me of the most profound truth of my whole life: Jesus loves me. It doesn't have to be complicated. We just have to be available to carry the wine and let others take a sip.

Sister, it's time to get ready for our wedding. It's coming and it's going to be the best wedding of all time when our Father hands Jesus His precious Bride. But we have a lot of invitations to get out before that day. I awoke one night from a deep sleep convinced that Jesus was asking me how I would live if He returned in two weeks. Our hour has indeed come to get ready (Revelation 19:7). It's time for a wedding.

I invite you into the same words the Holy Spirit spoke to my heart:

> Do you not think I can change the ordinary inside of you into the extraordinary for others? Do you not think I have enough to fill to the brim of your life—a life overflowing with new wine? You better believe I have saved the best

for now. This generation will serve the best wine, aged to perfection. Ages and generations of past revivals, miracles, wonders, and awakenings will not compare to what is about to released.

"'The days are coming,' declares the Lord, 'when the reaper will be overtaken by the plowman and the planter by the one treading grapes. New wine will drip from the mountains and flow from all the hills ... .'"
-Amos 9:13

Lord, would You fill "the overflow" in my life? Do the extraordinary. Do the impossible. Do the miraculous, and do it now, in Jesus' name.

Listen to this worship song: "Why Not Now" by Influence Music and Matt Gilman

Day Three

---✦---

REPENTANCE IS HERE

"In those days John the Baptist came, preaching in the wilderness of Judea and saying, 'Repent, for the kingdom of heaven has come near.'"
-Matthew 3:1-2

"From that time on Jesus began to preach, 'Repent, for the kingdom of heaven has come near.'"
-Matthew 4:17

I recently had a four-part dream about the Church. In the third part of my dream, I was watching a man dressed in a white suit leaning over an enormous white roulette table. As he threw the white ball on the round spinner and it bounced around, he said, "There have been many prophetic words spoken, but there is one people are not listening to. That word is 'repentance.'"

As I considered this dream, I questioned, "What are we missing or not hearing, Lord? What is in Your heart in revealing this word that's not landing?"

I have attempted to unwrap what God is speaking to His Bride right now. It comes with a sobriety in my heart for us.

- Repent was the first word of John the Baptist's gospel (Matthew 3:1-2).
- Repent was the first word of Jesus' gospel (Matthew 4:17).
- Repent was the first word of the twelve disciples preaching ministry (Mark 6:12).
- Repent was among the first words in the instructions Jesus gave to His disciples after His resurrection (Luke 24:46-47).
- Repent was the first word in Peter's word of exhortation in the first Christian sermon (Acts 2:38).
- Repent was the first word of Paul's ministry (Acts 26:19-20).

I have always struggled with the word "repent" because, in my mind, it carries the image of anger or wrath. Do this or else. Turn or burn. But what if that was never in God's heart in the first place. What if our English translation of the word is off from God's original intent?

Read the translation notes from the Mirror Bible:

> "The word 'repentance' is a fabricated word from the Latin word, penance, and to give religion more mileage the English word became re-penance! That is not what the Greek word means at all! The word, metanoia, comes from meta, together with and nous, mind or mental awareness. This word suggests a radical mind shift; it is to realize God's thoughts towards us. It is an awakening to the awareness of God's thoughts. To co-know."

God wants *metanoia* from us more than ever—to gather our thoughts around His thoughts in this hour more than ever. I believe He was inviting us from the very moment we encountered His goodness to begin to anchor our thoughts in His thoughts, His promises, and His character. Whether we are faced with difficult or painful experiences or growing in our identity in Him, it's critical to continue to anchor our lives in His thoughts toward us. Forever it will be a turning away from and an anchoring into Him. So beautiful and so safe.

> "What is meant [in repentance] is not a merely intellectual change of mind or mere grief, still less doing penance, but a fundamental turnaround involving mind and action and including overtones of grief, which assumes that human actions are fundamentally off course and need radical change.'" -D.A. Carson

> "To repent is not to feel bad but to think differently and therefore to act differently." -John Howard Yoder

There is an invitation to the fruitful life Christ has intended for you when He saved you by His grace. For example, because He sees me as holy, I can live in holiness. Because He calls me His beloved, I can love myself and love others. Our lives originate in God's thoughts toward us, and we live out of this truth and reality.

As believers, we have been clothed in the righteousness of Christ. He died the death we should have died. He took our sin and the wrath of God and bore it on the cross in our place. All of our sin, guilt, shame, accusation, and charges are wiped clean.

So how do believers repent? It boils down to this question: Are your thoughts and beliefs aligned with His? Ask Him. You will live out what you believe.

If John, Jesus, the disciples, and Paul all preached repentance, where have we backed down from this same message in the Church today? Where are we not aligning with the heart and thoughts of God toward lost people, fellow believers, or even toward ourselves?

God's heart is always love toward His people, but He also desires holiness and righteousness. The Church in America has lost her voice because of her great desire to not offend people, and it gave the enemy an open door to a spirit of fear. It's time to repent and get back to God's thoughts about you and me and the lost who don't know Him yet. We have to speak God's thoughts and not be silent.

> "Repentance in our time looks like this: We abandon methods that while good, would be a drag on revival. We examine crimes we have committed against the Holy Spirit and we forsake them. We end our theological apology tour. We look the culture right in the eye and say, 'I know you will hate me and say I am judgmental, but what I am about to tell you will bring life—life you never imagined.' And we prepare." -Mario Murillo[1]

We have much to return to as it pertains to God's original heart and purposes for the Church (as birthed in the book of Acts) and for us, as believers, when we were adopted as daughters. We were given a new identity and a new calling, commissioned to take the gospel forward from our very lives. His intent was that we believe Him and hold to His Word—His love letter revealing His passion for His people. If we are believing lies about the goodness of God, holiness, grace, and the truth of His promises, we need to return to His truth and His promises. We need to repent and realign with what we believe He says and hold fast to what is true.

> *"Timothy, guard what has been entrusted to your care. Turn away from godless chatter and the opposing ideas of what is falsely called knowledge, which some have professed and in so doing have departed from the faith. Grace be with you all."*
> -1 Timothy 6:20-21

In circling back to my dream, I want to beseech you to be available for the Lord to show you where you have come out of alignment with His heart and His truth. I believe God wants us to hit the jackpot on repentance so we can have the fullness of truth in our current reality. He wants us to know and live in the covenant He made to us in regard to abundance and His goodness. Would you dare to ask the Lord to search you and reveal any places where you need to return to His thoughts and align with what He is saying about you and others.

In all transparency, here are a few from my own from life:

- Lord, I have believed for too long that I am timid and afraid of mean people. I repent and come back to what you say of me. I am hidden in you and courageous because you live in me.
- Lord, I have bought the lie of the American dream for my comfort and my kingdom. I repent and ask you to build my life upon Your kingdom values and Your kingdom purposes.
- Lord, I have been waiting for the "next shoe to drop." I repent and return to your never ceasing goodness, faithfulness, and mercy. Help me align with your thoughts and promises for me.

"All those I dearly love I unmask and train. So, repent and be eager to pursue what is right. Behold, I'm standing at the door, knocking. If your heart is open to hear my voice and you open the door within, I will come in to you and feast with you, and you will feast with me."
-Revelation 3:19-20, TPT

Lord, return me to Yourself in the areas where I need realignment with Your heart. May I be available in every way to let You search me and return me to Your original intent for life in abundance with You.

Listen to this worship song: "Available" by Elevation Worship

Day Four

PURIFICATION AND INTIMACY

"Don't set the affections of your heart on this world or in loving the things of the world. The love of the Father and the love of the world are incompatible. For all that the world can offer us—the gratification of our flesh, the allurement of the things of the world, and the obsession with status and importance—none of these things come from the Father but from the world. This world and its desires are in the process of passing away, but those who love to do the will of God live forever."
-1 John 2:15-17, TPT

I believe we are in a very specific time of purification and intimacy by the hand and invitation of the Father. I write these words that I believe the Holy Spirit wants us to hear.

We are at a precipice. The Earth is shaking and trembling in fear. My people will begin to tremble in awe of Me. I will shake off fear. I will shake off complacency. To those who do not revere Me, I will shake the dust off My feet. Multitudes are in the valley of decision, but many are turning their hearts to begin to think about Me. For those who know Me, I implore them to not lose heart.

I am purifying My Bride (1 John 1:7). She has been purified by My blood and is being purified even now. The comforts and anchors of her heart to earthly things must be uprooted. For too long My people have placed their confidence in the things of the world they can see and hold on to. I am reestablishing their confidence in Me alone. This is the hour of intimacy and purity so that My Bride truly knows and follows Me. Her "love" is being tried and refined. I am OK with her struggle, questions, and doubt. We will drill down to the core of what each believes and what and who they love and follow. I am literally shaking them from the clutches of the enemy who has lied and lured them to captivity. I must gather My prized possession in this hour. There is a tearing away and a breaking off I have to do. I promise that disillusion will lead to depth; it will not result in despair or destruction. I will feed them the bread of Heaven to sustain them by My Spirit.

It is imperative you do not become weary or distracted. You cannot afford to meditate or dwell on negativity. That is not where I reside. To know Me is to know life. And to know Me is the most important thing. Intimacy and purification are the words of the hour. I am purifying My people from all ungodly connections and defamation (ungodly reputations). I am bringing them back into the truest sense of intimacy. But they also must be willing to let go of some things holding them captive. It's a time for complete honesty, transparency, and surrender before Me. No more playing religious games. No more loving Me and loving the things of the world. The decision is before My people just like I gave to Lot's wife. Will you forsake the cravings of the world for the cravings of Me?

I am getting the love of the world out of My people. I will instead replace it with a love for the world so they will be harvesters in My harvest field.

"And now, dear children, continue in him, so that when he appears we may be confident and unashamed before him at his coming."
-1 John 2:28

The purification process can be painful, but Jesus promises us a depth of intimacy if we will just let Him get to the roots of our affections. I believe this is our divine interruption, reset, return, revival for the Bride of Christ. This is just as important for us, His Bride, as it is for the harvest that is coming. He cares about the lost sheep, but He also cares deeply for the Bride He gave His very life for. We don't want to miss this moment, this precipice, this crossing over into greater intimacy and the fulfillment of many promises.

We have the invitation to run into greater freedom, intimacy, and power, right now. Come before the Lord in total transparency. Hold nothing back from His hand of healing. Ask Him:

Lord, are there places or things I'm holding onto where I love the world more than I love You? Holy Spirit, reveal the deepest recesses of my heart that need purification. I invite You to free me from anything that has held me captive.

Bring me into Your radical moves of freedom, deliverance, and healing. Where I am bound by fear of losing the comfort I find in the world, help me let go so I can trust You. Where I have struggled with disillusionment and doubt that You are good, give me faith to believe the truth. Where I am suffering through the purification process, give me endurance. Hover over me, Holy Spirit, as You did when You created the world. You hovered over the depths, and You spoke life. Speak new life into the places of my heart that need to be set free so I will only be a captive of the Lord Jesus Christ. You didn't give Your life so that I would share affections with You and the world.

Overwhelm me, Holy Spirit, Your anointed one, with the power of Your presence. Take this moment of surrender and multiply it into a life of passionate worship. Take my longing for freedom, healing, and deliverance and break every chain of captivity that binds me, in Jesus' name. I pray for a fresh surge of power to endure. May I run into the arms of intimacy, not looking back for a moment. Fix my eyes on You, Jesus. Release dreams and visions in this hour, in Your precious name. Amen.

Listen to this worship song: "Real Thing" by Maverick City Music featuring Dante Bowe

---
⚓

LOVE IS RETURNING

"In my distress I called to the Lord; I cried to my God for help. From his temple he heard my voice; my cry came before him, into his ears.

"The earth trembled and quaked, and the foundations of the mountains shook; they trembled because he was angry. Smoke rose from his nostrils; consuming fire came from his mouth, burning coals blazed out of it. He parted the heavens and came down; dark clouds were under his feet. He mounted the cherubim and flew; he soared on the wings of the wind. He made darkness his covering, his canopy around him—the dark rain clouds of the sky. Out of the brightness of his presence clouds advanced, with hailstones and bolts of lightning. The Lord thundered from heaven; the voice of the Most High resounded. He shot his arrows and scattered the enemy, with great bolts of lightning he routed them. The valleys of the sea were exposed and the foundations of the earth laid bare at your rebuke, Lord, at the blast of breath from your nostrils.

"He reached down from on high and took hold of me; he drew me out of deep waters. He rescued me from my powerful enemy, from my foes, who were too strong for me. They confronted me in the day of my disaster, but the Lord was my support. He brought me out into a spacious place; he rescued me because he delighted in me."
-Psalm 18:6-19

Love is returning, and in this season of challenges and heartaches, you need to hear the words: Love is returning to you all the enemy has taken. Love goes before you to revive things that need the life of Christ. We need to know that Love is returning for His people.

This portion of Psalm 18 was on my mind nonstop for weeks as I sensed strongly and with great sobriety the movement of God coming with His hand of justice and mercy. He has seen the affliction of His people across the Earth, and it has not been OK with Him. As we contended with the Lord in 2020, our cries went before Him. He heard every one of them. According to this passage in Psalm 18, there's a powerful response of God to the cries of His people as He hears us.

This is a psalm of great victory as David faced the reality of his enemy. But God does not sit silent or passive; He arises, and both David and the world encounter His power and deliverance. He thunders from Heaven and moves with accelerated speed on the *"wings of the wind (Psalm 18:10)."* Beloved, hold tight. He has not abandoned us.

There's been a deepening urgency in my heart that we, the Bride of Christ, would live with a revived fear of the Lord, coming out of the sheer knowledge and experience of His goodness and His power, His awe and wonder. There are things not in agreement with the heart of God right now across the Earth. If we are weeping regarding the injustice and evil happening across the globe, how much more the Lord is seeing and grieving. I must believe as we contend for God's heart to be released in the Earth, we must know His character and this glorious dimension of His justice and mercy, His judgment and love.

He loves the world He died for, and He is ever-committed to the preparation of His precious Bride He is coming back for.

I want to give you a soft and loving word of prophetic encouragement weighing heavy on my heart. This is what the Holy Spirit spoke to my heart for you:

> The enemy has overplayed his hand with My people. He has caused them to defile what once belonged to Me, in innocence and purity and holiness. And they handed it to him without reluctance. I am awakening My Bride to show them what they have handed over to him; they didn't even know they were doing it. I'm calling for holiness and purity in My people. They cannot look at the world any longer with a gaze of longing. I want My people to lay down all the places in their hearts—every one of their desires. Ask Me to sort them out. I want to expand, fulfill, and even remove some of them.

> *"Dear friends, now we are children of God, and what we will be has not yet been made known. But we know that when Christ appears, we shall be like him, for we shall see him as he is. All who have this hope in him purify themselves, just as he is pure."*
> -1 John 3:2-3

These are such crucial days of consecration. When Joshua called the people to break camp and cross over to the Promised Land, not everyone broke camp to leave with God's people; some stayed on the other side. Out of sheer disobedience they just didn't want to leave the familiar for what God had ahead of them. But the Lord is calling us to lay down our love and attention and affection on the edge of the wilderness for anything other than Christ Himself. We are moving into a new territory. There are two doors of invitation to us right now—the door of your heart and the door of Heaven.

"Behold, I'm standing at the door, knocking. If your heart is open to hear my voice and you open the door within, I will come in to you and feast with you, and you will feast with me."
-Revelation 3:20, TPT

"After this I looked, and there before me was a door standing open in heaven. And the voice I had first heard speaking to me like a trumpet said, 'Come up here, and I will show you what must take place after this.'"
-Revelation 4:1

Jesus stands at the door of our hearts, and it's our moment to ask Him to sort out every affection and attention of our lives. What do we hold so dearly that He wants placed in His hands? I had to sit with Him and bring Him every desire, longing, and passion for Him to expand, fulfill, and even remove. It was my moment of consecration with Him.

There's a second door before us, and it's an invitation to see things from Heaven's perspective. In both passages, Jesus doesn't come barging His way in. He is kind and patient, but He is also intimate and relational. And these two places of encounter are intimate invitations so we can walk in holiness and purity and purpose, bringing Heaven to Earth because we know the One our hearts adore, and He has taken up full residence.

Revival is coming to a people prepared to carry it.

The Church is awakening to her calling to demonstrate and proclaim the power and love of Christ. A world is awakening to the *"good news that will cause great joy for all the people (Luke 2:10b)."* We have been shaken so that we could not be moved. We are being prepared for a crossing over into a new era. God's people are being strengthened and stretched. And we will walk in a fear of the Lord in this next season as we see the hand of God move, the feet of God step into this chaos, and the voice of God thunder righteousness and deliverance. As the enemy overplays his hand, you better believe God is on His way. Love is returning.

> "Revival comes to turn us back, to restore our lives in God. This is God's central purpose, His number one priority: to make sure His Son has supremacy in our lives in all things." -Jeremiah Johnson

Take a moment before the Lord in consecration and invitation to ask God to do something intimate in your heart. Ask Him to ground you in a fear of the Lord. Then pray this prayer for endurance and increase and strengthening:

> Jesus, I stand before an open door of Heaven today and I ask You to take me higher in an intimate encounter with You to see Your preparation for the days ahead. I have been shaken but not moved because You are my strength, my rock, my fortress, my deliverer, my shield, my horn, my stronghold, and my strong God. You battle my enemies, and You deliver me from the grave.

> I pray, Lord, that I would be sober and joyously await Your power and wonder to astound me. I pray that every distraction and every affection for the world would fall at Your feet. Make for Yourself a holy and pure Bride, who knows only the love of the One my heart adores. Help me, as Your revivalist, walk in boldness and courage and a faith that is supernatural. I pray that as I stand on the shore of my promised land, face-to-face with my Promise Keeper, my heart would be secure in the love You have for me—an immovable love that knows no limitations.

Fall afresh on me, Holy Spirit, and let me walk about in peace through this world in turmoil because You have the final word. I join my voice with the four living creatures around the throne and declare, *"Holy, holy, holy, is the Lord God Almighty, who was, and is, and is to come (Revelation 4:8, ESV)."* Amen.

Listen to this worship song: "Revival's in the Air" by Dante Bowe

Day Six

---❧---

HERE I COME, JESUS

*"Then Jesus told his disciples a parable to show them
that they should always pray and not give up."*
-Luke 18:1

*"Then the Master said, 'Do you hear what that judge, corrupt as he is, is
saying? So what makes you think God won't step in and work justice for his
chosen people, who continue to cry out for help? Won't he stick up for them?
I assure you, he will. He will not drag his feet. But how much of that kind
of persistent faith will the Son of Man find on the earth when he returns?'"*
-Luke 18:6-8, MSG

*"'In my vision at night I looked, and there before me was one like a
son of man, coming with the clouds of heaven. He approached the
Ancient of Days and was led into his presence. He was given authority,
glory and sovereign power; all nations and peoples of every language
worshiped him. His dominion is an everlasting dominion that will not
pass away, and his kingdom is one that will never be destroyed.'"*
-Daniel 7:13-14

Do you think He's getting His sandals strapped back on?

I believe we are in a divine moment of God's goodness. It may not feel
like that in the natural when we look at the turmoil around us. But if

God's character, His ways, and His heart toward His people are always faithfulness, goodness, love, and mercy, this moment is not devoid of that reality. I believe this is our divine interruption, reset, returning, revival for the Bride of Christ.

My daughter, Lizzy, and I caught a friend on a walk one evening, and he shared what the Lord had been speaking. He said the Lord asked him, "What are you contending for right now?" As he spoke, my spirit leapt. The Lord hasn't called us to be reactionary in prayer, but to pray in the purposes and heart of God because we know the One we have loved and we know He is working to bring forth His heart in the world He gave His precious life for.

If Jesus is interceding for us—not in reaction but in preparation—what is He contending for as it pertains to His Bride? What do you think He is praying for us, His beautiful Bride?

This Scripture is continually in my heart, mind, and spirit.

> *"Let us rejoice and be glad and give him glory!*
> *For the wedding of the Lamb has come, and*
> *his bride has made herself ready."*
> -Revelation 19:7

In the waiting, Scripture indicates that many will lose heart and fall away in the days of trial and turmoil. We must guard against unbelief, fear, or begging like orphans in prayer. We are daughters who sit with Jesus in heavenly places (How glorious is that?) who have been adopted into royalty and, therefore, expect as daughters. God hears His people, loves them, cares for them, loves to bless them, and is always fair and merciful.

What has Jesus asked you to contend for in prayer until He returns? If God is the One who gives faith to us, is it currently activated and applied to everything, everyone, and every situation in my life? If He returned today, would He find me praying and living in expectation of Him?

> "God isn't just for you in some passive sense; God is for you in the most active sense imaginable. The Holy Spirit is praying hard for you. And supernatural synchronicities begin to happen when we tag-team with God and do the same." -Mark Batterson[2]

There's a rally cry across the Earth for us to contend for the most massive move of God history has seen. This is an hour of awakening to those who are perishing and for those who know Jesus but have made Him a side-dish to their lives. We must go on conquest for these two groups of people. Find them and call them to Jesus. Contend for them. Love them well without shame or judgment. Love them back to Jesus.

Be expectant. There are exploits assigned to you before the foundations of the world. Joan of Arc saved her nation because she heard the words of the Lord. She lost her life for being misunderstood by a culture that couldn't receive her. I have a sign in my house with one of her quotes, "I am not afraid. I was made for this." I pray you would carry an anointing of resolve, boldness, fearlessness, and faith as powerful as what she carried.

Arise, daughters of the Most High God. This is your hour of commissioning.

Listen to this worship song: "Forever Amen" by Steffany Gretzinger

CONSUME ME, JESUS

*"The earth was rocked at the sound of his voice from the mountain, but
now he has promised, 'Once and for all I will not only shake the systems
of the world, but also the unseen powers in the heavenly realm!'*

*"Now this phrase 'once and for all' clearly indicates the final removal of
things that are shaking, that is, the old order, so only what is unshakeable
will remain. Since we are receiving our rights to an unshakeable kingdom we
should be extremely thankful and offer God the purest worship that delights
his heart as we lay down our lives in absolute surrender, filled with awe.
For our God is a holy, devouring fire!"*
-Hebrews 12:26-29, TPT

Jesus is calling His Bride into a divine reset of our affections and attention to be entirely and completely on Him. That means fear has no right
to reside there; it must go. That means anger or frustration aren't invited
to the table any longer. Stress, anxiety, hopelessness, and fear of man are
uninvited guests in the home of our union and communion with Father,
Jesus, and Holy Spirit. Agitation, who made your bed in one of the rooms
of my heart?

The enemy will do everything in his power to keep our eyes on the shaking
and fill the rooms of our hearts with everything contrary to who God is.
Jesus wants to consume us with who He is. It's time for a house cleaning.

We are watching the literal shaking of world systems crumbling and being reset (fulfilling prophesy before our very eyes). Finance, government, religion, society are just a few things being shaken in this hour. But hear me. God's kingdom will not be shaken. He sits enthroned, not pacing Heaven. His Word is established, and it will be fulfilled. There is a destiny over your life, the Church, and our nation that God wants to see brought to completion. But I will boldly say, some things need to be shaken off and shaken loose for the kingdom of God to come and consume that space.

I was pondering this shaking and the changes I see happening with great acceleration and wondering if the fairy tale plans we all have of a "normal" life with work, family, retirement, and, well, the presumed American dream are no longer the course for us in America. What a mindset adjustment for us.

What if we have to take the American dream off the table entirely? But what if that trajectory was never the trajectory for the Bride anyway? What if we have been dulled by a plan that was not ever conceived in God's heart? Were we sold a treasure map that never promised the gold at the end of it all?

If we look at the infant Church as our road map, we find a sacred treasure map. They hid for fear of the Jews and were then consumed by tongues of fire and set out to take the gospel to the world. The Lord met them in their need for comfort and self-preservation with His great mercy. And He sent them running in zeal and passion for the movement of the gospel. They were indeed shaken, and they were indeed ignited with the awe and wonder and power of the Spirit.

The gospel spread like wildfire to both Jew and Gentile and from nation to nation. Believers were soaring in vision and power, miracles, and wonder. Yes, persecution preceded and followed them. Many lost their lives for the sake of the gospel. Some never even saw their promises fulfilled because the generations that followed them had to take up the mantle of calling and carry it. But when God showed up and called them to move, a fiery Church had its shoes on and its eyes fixed.

I have recently learned of several churches in the United States that will not gather corporately any longer. They are forming house churches (exactly like what God is doing all over the world with the Church). I believe these little house churches are forming in preparation for many things, one being little places of worship and discipleship for all the baby believers who will be found soon in the coming harvest—just like in the book of Acts. Let me remind you once again. There is a divine reset happening, and the purposes for the Bride of Christ will be fulfilled. And the best is yet to come.

> "But I leave you with a final challenge. What if the best churches haven't even been planted yet? What if the greatest sermons are yet to be preached? What if the best inventions, books, songs, and miracles are yet to come? I wouldn't doubt it. God always saves the best for last." -Mario Murillo[3]

Before we get to the best, it's just simply time to have a heart-to-heart conversation with the God of the universe who knows us so intimately (Psalm 139). It's time to invite Him to walk around the rooms of our hearts and clean house. Ask Him to shake off the very things that ensnare you and every wound that has pierced you (Hebrews 12:1). It's time to allow His Spirit to counsel us into complete truth and reveal every lie that is raising itself against the knowledge of God and the truth of His Word (2 Corinthians 10:5).

If He is going to shake all things and we know we are anchored in the love of Christ (Romans 8:37-39), we cannot be shaken. But the things that don't need to remain will be shaken indeed, and we can be confident that He has us. Don't fear the shaking. Rather, invite it. We need those things to go that inhabit us and are not of Jesus. They don't have a place in the life of a believer who is marked and sealed by Jesus, who carries His name and bears His victory and freedom.

Why do you believe they will never leave? Why do you fear you will be like this or live with this forever? Healing, deliverance, wholeness, strength, fortification, joy, hope, and victory are yours, in Christ Jesus. They are the very things that need to consume you—to fill every room of your heart. Even if you don't see the full manifestation here on Earth, this is your rightful inheritance because of the cross of Christ. Ask Him to fill you with these truths and realities that can't be shaken or removed. Fire of God, come and consume.

> Lord, help me come eye-to-eye and heart-to-heart with You. I pray for honesty and transparency to hear from You the things inhabiting my heart that need to go at the command of Your voice. Grant me courage to talk with You as You clean house—every room with no detail left unturned. As these things go, overwhelm me with awe, the fire of Your Spirit, and a fresh fear of the Lord, resulting in holiness and purity. I desire to experience Your presence and Your power to do in me what only You can do, intimate and full of Your goodness and wonder. May Your fire fall on me and send me running with the good news of Jesus far and wide. Raise me up as Your victorious one, fill my lamp with oil, and my mouth with praise. Bring miracles of deliverance and healing, Jesus. Come and touch me with a deep strengthening and resolve in my innermost being to trust and follow You. You are trustworthy and faithful to Your promises. Jesus, fill me with a greater measure of Your power and faith for the days ahead. Amen.

Listen to this worship song: "Have My Heart" by Maverick City Music

JESUS WILL ALWAYS COME FOR YOU

"When Mary finally found Jesus outside the village, she fell at his feet in tears and said, 'Lord, if only you had been here, my brother would not have died.'

"When Jesus looked at Mary and saw her weeping at his feet, and all her friends who were with her grieving, he shuddered with emotion and was deeply moved with tenderness and compassion. He said to them, 'Where did you bury him?'

"'Lord, come with us and we'll show you,' they replied.

"Then tears streamed down Jesus' face.

"Seeing Jesus weep caused many of the mourners to say, 'Look how much he loved Lazarus.' Yet others said, 'Isn't this the One who opens blind eyes? Why didn't he do something to keep Lazarus from dying?'

"Then Jesus, with intense emotions, came to the tomb—a cave with a stone placed over its entrance. Jesus told them, 'Roll away the stone.'

"Then Martha said, 'But Lord, it's been four days since he died—by now his body is already decomposing!'

*"Jesus looked at her and said, 'Didn't I tell you that if you
will believe in me, you will see God unveil his power?'*

*"So they rolled away the heavy stone. Jesus gazed into heaven and
said, 'Father, thank you that you have heard my prayer, for you
listen to every word I speak. Now, so that these who stand here with
me will believe that you have sent me to the earth as your messenger,
I will use the power you have given me.' Then with a loud voice
Jesus shouted with authority: 'Lazarus! Come out of the tomb!'*

*"Then in front of everyone, Lazarus, who had died four days
earlier, slowly hobbled out—he still had grave clothes tightly
wrapped around his hands and feet and covering his face!
Jesus said to them, 'Unwrap him and let him loose.'*

*"From that day forward many of those who had come to visit Mary believed
in him, for they had seen with their own eyes this amazing miracle! But
a few went back to inform the Pharisees about what Jesus had done."*
-John 11:32-46, TPT

Can you imagine what it felt like for Lazarus wondering, "Why has Jesus
healed so many and didn't show up for me?" Can you imagine his wres-
tling and disillusionment? As Lazarus was lying there, knowing Jesus was
in reach, and as he took his last breath, I wonder if he thought, "He never
came."

How many of us have thought these very words at different times? In a moment the thought quickly turns from a question to an accusation against
the very character of God.

**In our fragile state of dependency, we conclude
something concerning the faithfulness, love, protection,
or power of God. And the enemy laughs.**

If Satan can defame the character of God in the mind and life of a believer, he assumes victory.

But then came Jesus, full of compassion for not only Mary and Martha and those grieving but for Lazarus in his suffering and death. There was a grand testimony of God's love being written on many hearts as tear-filled eyes looked on. Jesus walked up to the grave of Lazarus and, with one statement, commanded Lazarus to walk out of the tomb. On the lips of Jesus was a declarative statement that Lazarus didn't have a choice to obey or to question. Jesus spoke to the power of death that held him back from life. Every knee in Heaven and on Earth will bow to Jesus—even death itself will bow its knee. And out walked a new man, wrapped in old grave clothes. His rags were not fit for this miracle of resurrection, so off they came. *"Unwrap him and let him loose (John 11:44, TPT)."* And a watching world saw first-hand what it looks like to receive new life as Christ gives it! It's miraculous and eternal, and death has zero say on those who are in Christ Jesus.

My husband, Mike, traveled to Amarillo, Texas, for work. When he arrived at the hotel, he noticed a large moving van. Since Amarillo is the halfway point to many destinations, it's not uncommon that people take a break there overnight. Two days later the moving van was still there. As Mike was standing in the lobby, in shuffled a very sad man. My husband made his way to the front desk to ask if this man was OK. The lady at the front desk shared that this man and his wife had all their possessions in the truck and were en route to a new home. The wife had a medical emergency and died in the ambulance the day before, and he had to wait for her ashes to be ready. Can you imagine the depth of pain and disillusionment the man felt? This was his Lazarus moment—waiting for a miracle that never came, at least at this stage of his journey, on this page of the chapter. So off he drove to his new home with his wife's ashes in an urn.

Jesus defied the power of the grave over Lazarus because He could—four days after Lazarus died. In the story above, we would assume Jesus didn't come for that desperate man because his wife didn't come back to life. But we only see from our earthly perspective. We don't see the miracle God will do and is planning to do in this man's desperation. God is a wonder-working God who puts His love and power continually on display to draw all men to himself. In this world we will have many troubles, but Jesus said, *"I have overcome the world (John 16:33)."* I believe Jesus will show Himself to this man in a way only He knows how to do.

Beloved, I want you to know that, no matter what, Jesus is coming for you. There is nothing He cannot do for you. Nothing withholds His demonstrative love to His people. He has come, and He has rescued you from the grip of death; it has no power over you. It is not the final word over your life. His resurrection life is the final word over you. You were buried with Him and raised with Him. This is a present and an eternal reality. You can live like Paul when he said:

> *"However, I consider my life worth nothing to me; my only aim is to finish the race and complete the task the Lord Jesus has given me—the task of testifying to the good news of God's grace."*
> - Acts 20:24

Or when he wrote:

> *"I eagerly expect and hope that I will in no way be ashamed, but will have sufficient courage so that now as always Christ will be exalted in my body, whether by life or by death. For to me, to live is Christ and to die is gain."*
> -Philippians 1:20-21

Jesus will always come. It's who He is. He is faithful even when we don't think He is. I implore you in these days of division, disillusionment, discord, and doubt, to remain faithful to the One you have entrusted your very life to. He will never abandon or forsake you, even if you are staring at a grave right in the face. He will carry you from glory to glory; that's His promise.

> Lord Jesus, give faith to eyes and ears. Faith that comes by seeing You move on our behalf and ears that hear Your words of life and comfort to those in valleys of pain or praise. I pray for an anointing of a greater deposit of belief, trust, and resolve that You are for us and not against us. I pray we would declare You are indeed a miracle-working God and hold on to that truth against all odds. Release miracles, Lord, in the lives of my sister today, in Jesus' name.

Listen to this worship song: "You Came" by Jonathan and Melissa Helser

YOUR VOICE IS BEING RESTORED

"'Truly I tell you, if anyone says to this mountain, "Go, throw yourself into the sea," and does not doubt in their heart but believes that what they say will happen, it will be done for them.'"
-Mark 11:23

"Then he said to me, 'Prophesy to the breath; prophesy, son of man, and say to it, "This is what the Sovereign Lord says: Come, breath, from the four winds and breathe into these slain, that they may live."' So I prophesied as he commanded me, and breath entered them; they came to life and stood up on their feet—a vast army."
-Ezekiel 37:9-10

"In the beginning God created the heavens and the earth. Now the earth was formless and empty, darkness was over the surface of the deep, and the Spirit of God was hovering over the waters. And God said, 'Let there be light,' and there was light."
-Genesis 1:1-3

"For you can all prophesy in turn so that everyone may be instructed and encouraged."
-1 Corinthians 14:31

"The disciples went and woke him, saying, 'Master, Master, we're going to drown!' He got up and rebuked the wind and the raging waters; the storm subsided, and all was calm."
-Luke 8:24

"'Even on my servants, both men and women, I will pour out my Spirit in those days, and they will prophesy.'"
-Acts 2:18

The Holy Spirit prompted a prophetic word in my heart to speak over the Bride:

> My people need their voice back. The enemy has tried to take the voice of My Bride—to muzzle her. But she has to proclaim My life, My light, My words of truth to this devastated world. There will come a grieving for being silent because many will feel they missed their opportunity. They will grieve their own silence. My grace will give them back their voice, and they will speak with even greater resolve and conviction. Boldness will arise in them. My Church will not be silent any longer. She will not just sit back and let life happen. My people are called to change atmospheres, cultures, cities, neighborhoods, generations. I am restoring her voice. She will no longer bow her knee to fear of man, fear of offending, or fear of rejection. She will speak to culture, and her voice will create life, usher in freedom, and bring deliverance. The voice of the Bride and the Bridegroom will be united. They will speak as one because she will know the word of the Lord. The Bride of Christ will get loud. She will declare life. She will declare deliverance and salvation and declare prison doors to open. She will not be mute any longer.

Did you know that on the Hebrew calendar, 2020 was the year of the mouth? Interesting and symbolic that it was also the year of covering the mouth. But I believe with all my heart the Bride of Christ has a voice that needs to speak to darkness, prison doors, and to spiritually dead and hurting people. We have an opportunity to get bold in intercession before the throne of God, but we also have the words of life inside us. The Church will not be silenced. The Bride has a love letter and a sword to wield. It's time, dear sister, to pray and declare and announce the words of the Lord.

Several women have said, "Jules, I just don't hear the voice of God. How do I speak His heart when I can't discern His voice?" Beloved, hide His Word inside you, and you will hear His voice. This is the beginning place of discerning His voice. If it aligns with what you know about Him, it's probably His voice. And when He speaks, confirm it with Scripture, and don't be paralyzed by analysis. Receive the words, let the Holy Spirit bring the confirmation to your spirit, and open your mouth. God's words to you will be consistent with His Word. They will never contradict themselves. His voice is the most familiar voice to you because He is the most communicative God. Trust me, He is speaking to you, and He will speak through you. But you must open your mouth.

There are things in the natural that need you to speak life. Just like the Lord told Ezekiel, prophesy life to those dead bones. We get to speak life, blessing, healing, and victory over ourselves, other people, our work, our marriages, the Bride of Christ, our cities, etc. When the angel of the Lord encountered Gideon hiding, what did he declare of him? He called him a "mighty warrior," who he was in the spirit. He was hiding in fear in a winepress, not the place you'd find a warrior. We must begin to declare things from God's perspective—what He sees and what He believes about people and situations. There is power in our spoken words, dear sister.

I love this decree written by Lana Vawser in her book "The Prophetic Voice of God." Say it out loud with me:

"I am an overcomer in Jesus's name. I am seated in heavenly places with Christ Jesus. I engage with the Word of God and His promises over my life. I am a mouthpiece who decrees blessing and life and not death. I decree that in my process, right now, that God's promises over my life are true, no matter what my eyes see. I decree that I trust in God and what He has spoken to me, and I will remain engaged in His Word and what He has spoken to me in Jesus's name."[4]

In the beginning, the Trinity was hovering over darkness where life had yet to be created, and God spoke things into existence. Jesus looked at the storm and commanded it to be still. Ezekiel called forth an army with his voice. Jesus called Lazarus from death to life with His voice. There is power in our voice when God puts the word of the Lord on your tongue—life is created. So let's go together boldly before the throne of grace. It's time for the Lord to restore your voice, strengthen your faith and your boldness, and pour out His Spirit on you to prophesy (speak the revealed words of God). Here's a few things that come to mind immediately:

- Take this moment to declare His promises over your marriage.
- Perhaps you are in need of healing. Speak the living Word of God over your health and your body. Get those Scriptures of healing and speak them to yourself out loud.
- With your voice, call your prodigals home.
- If there's a storm in your finances, your home, your relationships, your thought life, it's time to command it to be still. Every spirit must bow at the name of Jesus.
- Are your children wandering, confused, distracted? Declare the name of Jesus over them. What are the promises God has given you regarding your children?
- Will you decree that the Church in America and around the globe is awakening to the true gospel, one ablaze with the glory of God!

Let me pray over you:

> Lord, I pray for the one who has felt she has either lost her voice or has been muzzled. Set her free, give her boldness to speak, and freedom from a fear of rejection or a fear of man. I pray she will utter the words of the Lord with great humility and confidence she hears from You. I pray the fire of God would touch her tongue and anoint her words to pray Heaven to Earth and to speak life into existence. I pray her words are filled with faith and vision, resolve and conviction. Lord, out of Your mercy, move her from silence to boldness, by the power of Your Spirit. Thank You for Your counsel, Your Word, Your words by the Spirit, and Your friendship to those who walk with You intimately. Increase her longing for You and a passion to hide Your Word in her heart. Awaken an army of women to arise in this hour, Lord, who have the word of the Lord on their lips. And assemble us together by Your Spirit, in Jesus' name! God Almighty declares the word of the gospel with power, and the warring women of Zion deliver its message. Do it, Lord, for Your name's sake and for Your glory!

Listen to this worship song: "Prophesy" by Influence Music featuring Melody Noel

---✦---

RAISE YOUR EBENEZER

"So Samuel said to all the Israelites, 'If you are returning to the Lord with all your hearts, then rid yourselves of the foreign gods and the Ashtoreths and commit yourselves to the Lord and serve him only, and he will deliver you out of the hand of the Philistines.' So the Israelites put away their Baals and Ashtoreths, and served the Lord only.

"Then Samuel said, 'Assemble all Israel at Mizpah, and I will intercede with the Lord for you.' When they had assembled at Mizpah, they drew water and poured it out before the Lord. ...

"While Samuel was sacrificing the burnt offering, the Philistines drew near to engage Israel in battle. But that day the Lord thundered with loud thunder against the Philistines and threw them into such a panic that they were routed before the Israelites. The men of Israel rushed out of Mizpah and pursued the Philistines, slaughtering them along the way to a point below Beth Kar.

"Then Samuel took a stone and set it up between Mizpah and Shen. He named it Ebenezer, saying, 'Thus far the Lord has helped us.'"
-1 Samuel 7:3-6a, 10-12

The Israelites were again standing in a familiar place face-to-face with their enemy, the Philistines. They had been defeated once before in this place called Mizpah. Now the prophet Samuel was leading them. But Samuel had a new plan from the Lord. It would not require battle tactics or military strategy. God was going right for the heart of the matter. He wanted to show them the ultimate victory and the true battle: the battle for their affections. So Samuel called the nation of Israel to repentance and returning. This would be an internal working of their hearts and an external expression of their devotion. It was time to clean house and get rid of the additional gods they worshipped. God was doing a realignment from the inside out. And indeed, He would mark this moment with His mighty roar, victory, deliverance, and restoration.

Samuel not only called the children of Israel to repentance but also to a singular focus; it was time to serve God and God alone. For too long, their affections and actions had been clouded with blending a little of this and a little of that till the lines were blurred and the enemy ran rampant. It was another Joshua moment for the people of God: *"'… choose this day whom you will serve … (Joshua 24:15, ESV).'"*

> "But a worse enemy than the Philistines held sway over the land. … The people were thus in double bondage; the heavy yoke of the Philistines was upon them, because the heavier burden of a false worship crushed out the life of their hearts." -Charles Spurgeon

So the people assembled and took down their physical gods of worship, their poles and Baals. Samuel then stood in the gap for his nation in a place of intercession. In this town of Mizpah, where they had been defeated before, Samuel prayed to God. It was a moment when their repentance was ready to encounter the intervention from Heaven. Samuel drew deep water and poured it out, demonstrating the depth of their confession being poured before the Lord. It was a beautiful expression of emptiness and need being poured out—not one last drop reserved but all of it poured out.

"Arise, cry out in the night, as the watches of the night begin;
pour out your heart like water in the presence of the Lord."
-Lamentations 2:19a

I believe our pouring out of the deepest things within us is often a precursor to victory. As I was writing this devotional, I had to pour out my heart before the Lord, to get honest before Him so together we could bring the deep places of our heart to Him for His counsel and His healing touch. Often getting to this place of honesty and emptying is the victory. That day, the Israelites had a process the Lord was taking them through to get to freedom and wholeness. Samuel stood in the gap for his nation and dared to call the children of Israel back to the Lord, but they also had to be willing. God heard the intercession, smelled the burnt offering of an innocent baby lamb, and responded to the distress of His people. A mighty roar from Heaven came forth.

> "The eyes of the Lord see everything but they focus on what is going on with His people. Let us come before Him now, aware of our total helplessness. Let us announce that we are His people and that we do not fear our time, but we fear the Lord, and we have come to stand before His presence on behalf of a new demonstration of His glory on earth." -Mario Murillo[5]

The people of Israel longed ultimately for deliverance from their enemy. God did that in a second. But what was more important to the Lord was their hearts of worship. False gods, ideologies, perversions, and idolatry had crept in. I'm sure it was subtle, just one little thing and then another. And before they knew it, God's people were in captivity worshipping everything that was not of the true living God. And a man of God dares to call them back and dares to stand in the gap for his nation, serving as a prophet, intercessor, and warrior.

I believe the Lord is calling His Bride to this very place to call our nations back to Him.

A mighty thunderous roar routed the enemy of the people of God that day. He sent the enemy into confusion and retreat. And the people of God slaughtered their enemy and never saw their invasion again. Both the Israelites and the Philistines heard the Lord's roar that day. What caused confusion in one caused confidence to arise in God's people. Then the Lord did something so beautiful for His own—he restored and brought full deliverance from the authority and presence of the enemy in their lives.

Where does victory begin? It begins with our hearts being poured out before the Lord. It's time to get honest with ourselves before Him—pour it all out—because there's victory waiting for the people of God. If the cross was sufficient for our healing, freedom, and deliverance because of the death and resurrection of Jesus, you better believe He's roaring for His people to awaken and shake loose anything that is not of Him.

In response, Samuel raised an Ebenezer before the Lord. This was an altar of remembrance. The name Ebenezer means "stone of help," and it was a reminder to the people of the hand of the Lord moving on their behalf. No longer would their eyes see altars of Baal or Ashtoreth poles; their eyes would see an altar of worship to the Most High God, worthy of their praise and affections.

> "He redeems us that we might worship again, that we might take our place again, even on earth with the angels in heaven, and the beasts and the living creatures. That we might feel in our hearts and express in our own way that humbling but nevertheless delightful sense of admiring awe and astonished wonder and overwhelming love—in the presence of that ancient mystery, that unspeakable majesty, that Ancient of Days." -A.W. Tozer[6]

Sister, it's time to raise your Ebenezer, your stone of remembrance, and bring to mind your first Love when He was the only thing that consumed your heart and mind.

When the Lord led me to 1 Samuel 7, I had no idea what He was about to drop in my spirit. But that same call to the Israelites in that day is His call to the Bride of Christ. It is time to return and set all our affections on Christ alone. Oh, that we would not be double minded any longer, pursuing God and pursuing the things of the world. He's looking in this hour for sold-out, laid-down, surrendered worshippers who have climbed up on the altar and asked to be a living sacrifice, holy and pleasing to the Lord (Romans 12:1). Pour it out, sister, every last drop at His feet, just like Mary did (John 12:3). Her most costly gifts laid at the feet of Jesus in worship. Then take that broken jar and let it be your Ebenezer. Fill your journal with the words of God to you—let that be your Ebenezer. Look at the women in your boat who are with you as you push off from shore into deeper waters and build that altar of remembrance together. We have to remind ourselves when the squalls rise that He has been faithful, and He will be faithful again.

As we moved with God's people from repentance to intercession to victory to restoration and finally deliverance, look at 1 Samuel 7:14: *"The towns from Ekron to Gath that the Philistines had captured from Israel were restored to Israel, and Israel delivered the neighboring territory from the hands of the Philistines. And there was peace between Israel and the Amorites."*

After God restored His people to what was rightfully theirs, they became deliverers for those who were also oppressed. The Lord will use your deliverance from the enemy to deliver others. Nothing will be wasted. And like He promised, He will *"repay you for the years the locusts have eaten … (Joel 2:25)."*

What we pour out, He will turn and use it to bring forth life. Nothing will be wasted. Watch and see. We cannot out pour God.

> *"'For I will pour water on the thirsty land, and streams on the dry ground; I will pour out my Spirit on your offspring, and my blessing on your descendants. They will spring up like grass in a meadow, like poplar trees by flowing streams.'"*
> -Isaiah 44:3-4

Listen to this worship song: "Egypt" by Bethel Music featuring Cory Asbury

Day Eleven

FAITH AND GRATITUDE: THE GREAT HINGE

"Now on his way to Jerusalem, Jesus traveled along the border between Samaria and Galilee. As he was going into a village, ten men who had leprosy met him. They stood at a distance and called out in a loud voice, 'Jesus, Master, have pity on us!'

"When he saw them, he said, 'Go, show yourselves to the priests.' And as they went, they were cleansed.

"One of them, when he saw he was healed, came back, praising God in a loud voice. He threw himself at Jesus' feet and thanked him—and he was a Samaritan.

"Jesus asked, 'Were not all ten cleansed? Where are the other nine? Has no one returned to give praise to God except this foreigner?' Then he said to him, 'Rise and go; your faith has made you well.'"
-Luke 17:11-19

As they went, Jesus and His disciples encountered a group of outcast, suffering, and very sick lepers. I did a little research on leprosy. Dr. Allen L. Gillen writes:

"Its symptoms start in the skin and peripheral nervous system (outside the brain and spinal cord), then spread to other parts, such as the hands, feet, face, and earlobes. Patients with leprosy experience disfigurement of the skin and bones, twisting of the limbs, and curling of the fingers to form the characteristic claw hand. Facial changes include thickening of the outer ear and collapsing of the nose. ... The leprosy bacillus destroys nerve endings that carry pain signals; therefore patients with advanced leprosy experience a total loss of physical pain. When these people cannot sense touch or pain, they tend to injure themselves or be unaware of injury caused by an outside agent."

We see these ten lepers who encountered Jesus, and somehow they knew Him. His reputation preceded Him, perhaps. There was an authority about this man, and they wanted His pity. In Jesus' compassion, He had far more to give them than just pity. (It makes me think of how often I come into contact with a sick person and only extend them pity or compassion when I've got Jesus, who longs to heal them, living in me.) The Son of God, whose very presence and power comes with great authority, told them to go. And as they went, healing came to these ten suffering lepers. One step of faith and then another step. Did the feeling start coming back in their nervous system? Did their bones begin to untwist or their limbs grow back? Perhaps they watched one another as the healing power of Heaven touched them. Can you even imagine the wonder in their eyes?

The story could have stopped here, and we would still marvel at the wonder of God through the life of Christ. But I believe the story hinges on one thing. The most catalytic point of this entire encounter is about to be made.

"One of them, when he saw he was healed, came back, praising God in a loud voice. He threw himself at Jesus' feet and thanked him—and he was a Samaritan."
-Luke 17:15-16

One physically healed leper came back with a mouthful of praise and gratitude for the One who literally changed his reality. The others were probably celebrating and testifying, but one came back to the source of his healing and, in total worship, fell at Jesus' feet. Defying all cultural barriers, this Samaritan fell at the feet of a Jewish man. This whole story is hinged on this one moment of gratitude. It changed everything for this one leper. Jesus not only healed him physically; He was about to heal his heart and make him whole. No longer would he be a leper or an orphan.

"Then Jesus said to the healed man lying at his feet, 'Arise and go. It was your faith that brought you salvation and healing.'"
-Luke 17:19, TPT

Jesus touched the man's life just as he asked, but He had much more He could do in the former leper's heart that would impact his eternity. This man had a heart positioned before God to touch and invade. It was his gratitude that set the table for God to come and dine. He left the presence of Jesus forever changed. Jesus had so much to work with as it pertained to the man's heart, which all hinged on faith and gratitude. He was rescued, saved, and made whole from this place of worship.

I had a defining moment in 2013 as I sat with my pastor friend, Mike O'Rand. I was metaphorically writhing in pain from a long season of hardship. I authentically shared the feelings of disappointment and dis-illusionment with God. He looked at me and said, "We don't determine when our season of suffering ends. Look at the life of David as he was prepared to be king. You need to stop complaining and just praise Him and thank Him. Take the next 60 days, and do not ask for one thing. Just praise Him." That is exactly what I did. I praised Him and thanked Him for every little thing. My perspective began to change; my family began to live and speak and create an atmosphere of gratitude. And hands down, I can tell you, this shifted the trajectory of our season.

Gratitude was the hinge for us moving from one season to another. But more than that, my heart was set free.

So dear sister, no matter what disfigurement, suffering, hardship, or pain you are experiencing, you always have the choice to go to Jesus and fall at His feet and praise Him. It becomes the very thing that changed everything (for eternity) for this one leper. Jesus delights in process, and He works on multiple levels of our lives. He wants our healing physically emotionally, mentally, and especially spiritually. He wants our wholeness, and He paid to provide it.

As you go, take one step of faith and then another. As you go, praise Him—fall at His feet in worship. As you go, take the power and the presence of Jesus to dying and destitute people because you have more to give them than pity; you have the God of the impossible living inside you.

> Jesus, I pray for the fire of Your presence to fall on my sister. Show her the places You long to bring healing in her heart and life. You are roaring from Heaven on her behalf, that she would run in freedom and wholeness. I pray for the gift of faith to believe You for impossible things. I pray for her mouth to be filled with praise for the One her heart adores. I pray You would free her from any lies the enemy has told her that "This is how it will always be." Lord, release healing and wholeness to her heart, body, mind, emotions, relationships, and family. May these 40 days of intimacy and encounter catapult her into all that is on

Your heart for her. Bring it forth in fullness and victory, in Jesus' name!

Listen to this worship song: "Thank You" by Maverick City Music featuring Steffany Gretzinger and Chandler Moore

---♣---

HE'S DONE EVERYTHING WELL

*"Then Jesus left the vicinity of Tyre and went through Sidon,
down to the Sea of Galilee and into the region of the Decapolis.
There some people brought to him a man who was deaf and could
hardly talk, and they begged Jesus to place his hand on him.*

*"After he took him aside, away from the crowd, Jesus put his fingers
into the man's ears. Then he spit and touched the man's tongue. He
looked up to heaven and with a deep sigh said to him, 'Ephphatha!'
(which means 'Be opened!'). At this, the man's ears were opened,
his tongue was loosened and he began to speak plainly.*

*"Jesus commanded them not to tell anyone. But the more he did
so, the more they kept talking about it. People were overwhelmed
with amazement. 'He has done everything well,' they said.
'He even makes the deaf hear and the mute speak.'"*
-Mark 7:31-37

This man's miracle started with the faith of his friends.

Jesus walked about 50 miles to get to this region and encounter this
man who needed a miracle. It wasn't a waste of time or energy for Jesus.
This deaf and mute man was worth all the miles He trod in His sandals
on that dusty road. And the risky faith of this man's friends was worth

their possibility of disappointment. They stepped into a moment to bring Heaven to Earth.

Jesus encountered this man's friends bringing him from their own place of longing and desperation. These friends were begging Jesus to do something only He could do. There is nothing like friends who bring you to the feet of Jesus. He knows no limitations on receiving us, so we should have no limitations in bringing one another to Him for healing. Together in that place, we both become undone with the power and the wonder of God.

During a mission trip to Fort Hood, I (and two others) had the joy of bringing my dear friend and her brother to the feet of Jesus. Our room of four awoke one night to a call of sheer sadness and grief as this woman's brother was unexpectedly in the intensive care unit. Three of us encircled her and worshipped and prayed and read the Word of God over her brother and the situation for more than two hours. It was a sacred moment. The next day, in the midst of her own suffering, we went out into the harvest field, and I watched the spirit of God rise up in her to declare the gospel message. Five high school boys accepted Christ as their Savior in just a matter of minutes of hearing about the love of Jesus. I don't know if I have ever seen the redemption of God come with such acceleration and vindication in just hours. Jesus will have the final word on life and death. Five were snatched from Hell that day, as we continued to pray for the miracle of recovery for her brother. I can say with utter conviction: Jesus indeed has the final word!

Back to the man seeking healing. Before Jesus stood a man who could neither hear nor speak. Jesus pulled him aside to be eye to eye with Him, probably within in a stone's throw of the friends and onlookers. I see the love of Christ protecting this man's dignity, not making a spectacle out of his brokenness. Then He proceeded to do something unique with the man. The method of His healing is not anything we have seen Jesus do in the Gospels before. He used a new method. He could speak a word, but the man would not hear. He did something that would demonstrate His understanding and intimacy in a way that this man could comprehend!

> "Many people cared about this man, and perhaps many had prayed for his healing. But no one ever stuck their fingers in his ears and spit on his tongue like this. Jesus did something completely new to catch this man's attention because He could not catch his attention with words." -David Guzik, Mark 7 commentary

> "Through touch and the use of spittle Jesus entered into the mental world of the man and gained his confidence." -William Lane, Mark 7 commentary

Jesus is so intimate, so personal, so kind, and so attentive.

As He placed His fingers in the man's ears and places His spit upon the man's tongue, He lifted His head to Heaven and sighed. This sigh indicates not only His compassion for the man but the deep grief of the sin of this broken world. And then He prayed to His Father. The Greek word for "sigh" is the same word used in Romans 8:22-23 where we "groan" for what we don't not yet have: full redemption.

> *"We know that the whole creation has been groaning as in the pains of childbirth right up to the present time. Not only so, but we ourselves, who have the firstfruits of the Spirit, groan inwardly as we wait eagerly for our adoption to sonship, the redemption of our bodies. For in this hope we were saved. But hope that is seen is no hope at all. Who hopes for what they already have?"*
> -Romans 8:22-24

Jesus was getting ready to pay for brokenness with His very life. We were, in part, the joy set before Him as He endured that cross. The victory, freedom, and healing that came forth is not a theological idea but a profound reality that is ours to take hold of. Oh, that we would be the ones who declare freedom to the captives and healing to the brokenhearted.

Jesus lifted His head, looked to Heaven, and called for the Father to move on behalf of this broken man. This moment is a direct fulfillment prophesied of Jesus.

"Then will the eyes of the blind be opened and the ears of the deaf unstopped. Then will the lame leap like a deer, and the mute tongue shout for joy. Water will gush forth in the wilderness and streams in the desert."
-Isaiah 35:5-6

The Messiah has come. And as the people gazed on at the miraculous healing of the deaf and mute man, the crowds declared in awe and wonder, *"He has done everything well ... He even makes the deaf hear and the mute speak (Mark 7:37)."* And suddenly that deaf, mute man had a mouth full of wonder to declare things he was never able to articulate before. Jesus gave this man a new testimony that no one could argue with.

Here are a few things we can count on from this encounter:

- He does do all things well. The work of redemption in our lives is done oh so well. He is trustworthy in all His ways, even when we don't understand the process. But the process is as glorious to Him as the end result.
- As much as Jesus and the Father were critical to this man's healing, so were his friends. It is urgently important that we are surrounded with people who are going to steer, move, and sometimes carry us to Jesus. When we don't have faith, we need the strength and faith of those who will run us right to that throne of grace.
- Jesus will always be intimate in His approach and unique in His process. He doesn't work by method nor does He expect us to. When we pray for healing for someone, every time may look

different. That is just the creativity and intimacy of Christ in and through us to a hungry, hurting world. We get to approach people with freedom as we minister in the power and authority of Christ in us, not by law or rule or method.

I want to prophesy to you that He will do all things well in your life. Those who stand with you will receive a deeper conviction of the power of the love and goodness of God! My heart was expanded as I watched my dear friend walk through the valley of the shadow of death just hours earlier and courageously declare the salvation of Jesus with eyes heavy from tears a few hours later. And five men's lives will never be the same. If I could look at you with eyes of compassion as some of you are just in hard spaces in life, I would tell you that your firm anchor in Christ is immovable. He will carry you through this process, and I promise that one day you will have full understanding. And one day you will praise God for this storm.

> So, Lord, fortify my sister with friends who will walk her right to You every time. When she feels lonely, send new friends who are passionate for you. Give her tenacity in the process requiring faith—to believe You to be who You say You are and do what You promised You will do. I ask for anointing of faith to be deposited in her. Give her faith for impossibility. Strengthen her in the secret place as she waits on You. Renew her as she worships and clings to You with all she has. I pray the joy of the Lord to revive her weary and tired heart. Raise her up to declare the goodness and the wonder of God. Loosen her tongue to speak and her ears to hear what You are speaking today. In the mighty and wondrous name of Jesus, amen!

Listen to this worship song: "Every Victory" by The Belonging Co, Danny Gokey

Day Thirteen

---◆---

OUR HAGGAI MOMENT

"'Is it a time for you yourselves to be living in your paneled houses, while this house remains a ruin?'"
-Haggai 1:4

"This is what the Lord Almighty says: 'Give careful thought to your ways. Go up into the mountains and bring down timber and build my house, so that I may take pleasure in it and be honored,' says the Lord."
-Haggai 1:7-8

"Then Haggai, the Lord's messenger, gave this message of the Lord to the people: 'I am with you,' declares the Lord. So the Lord stirred up the spirit of Zerubbabel son of Shealtiel, governor of Judah, and the spirit of Joshua son of Jozadak, the high priest, and the spirit of the whole remnant of the people. They came and began to work on the house of the Lord Almighty, their God ... ."
-Haggai 1:13-14

I woke up one morning with these words in my spirit: "It's a Haggai moment!" I love those minor prophets of the Old Testament but needed to dive into the book of Haggai to see what God was saying. It's a beautiful word of redirection, correction, hope, and vision to us. Much in the Church is being shaken, shifted, and flipped right side up. The Bride is getting her voice back. People are seeing harvest fields and stepping into personal revival. The Church is beginning to decide how strong (in faith and resolve) she will swim across the current of culture and stand for the truth of God and His Word. It's hard and glorious and eternal.

The goodness of the Lord is revealed to Haggai in His words spoken to the remnant (about 50,000 people) who had returned from Babylon. They were a people who had lived in a culture for 70 years whose motto was, "I am, and there is none besides me." They were facing a drought at the time, and perhaps God had His people's attention. There they were, generations later, back in the Promised Land and being called to throw off building their own kingdoms to build His kingdom. But what He was asking them was wrapped in the promise of what was yet to appear: His coming glory.

The words of God don't come with condemnation but rather correction through Haggai, causing the people to pause and reflect. The people had been building beautiful homes for themselves, focused on their own individual lives and pursuits. Meanwhile, the house of the Lord—the place where God's presence and glory dwelt—was in ruins. But what did God remind His people? He had the heart to heart with them but reminded them of His presence with them. He wasn't forsaking them in their double-mindedness or self-focus. He wasn't going anywhere. *"I am with you,"* He said.

After He spoke, the people began to work, and while they worked, the Lord continued to be with them. But there is silence for a month. Some things needed to settle in their hearts perhaps; a redirection needed to happen in their focus and desire.

Silence isn't rejection; sometimes it shapes noise.

Things had to be set right in God's people. They were asked to forsake the things they had known culturally from Babylon and return to the Lord to build His house so His glory could come. How He longed for intimacy with them and for them to know their God and to partner with His purposes. So He sent a prophet of purity to redirect the people in the more of what He had for them.

I penned these words in my journal as I sat with the Lord:

> I am looking, watching, and waiting to find those whose hearts are entirely devoted to Me. I don't want a divided heart in My people. I want a heart whose purposes are in direct alignment with Me. I am the foundation of their lives—nothing else but Me. Will I find those burning ones? Will My people emerge from the fire, refined and delivered or covered in soot? Will these ones set their faces like flint toward Heaven or sit in self-pity and self-consumption, bitter and ungrateful? Each one is given a choice to return to Me, but not all will. I know many do not want My fire to burn in them. They want comfort, and they want the world. Those who build their life on Me will see Me with them, and My Spirit will come. My blessing will come. If Christ is not the foundation, the foundation will crumble.

Those who remained in Babylon were still God's people, but only the remnant left and followed God into His greater purposes. Everyone received the invitation, but not everyone responded.

> *"Jesus replied: 'A certain man was preparing a great banquet and invited many guests. At the time of the banquet he sent his servant to tell those who had been invited, "Come, for everything is now ready." But they all alike began to make excuses. The first said, "I have just bought a field, and I must go and see it. Please excuse me."*

*"Another said, "I have just bought five yoke of oxen, and
I'm on my way to try them out. Please excuse me."*

"'Still another said, "I just got married, so I can't come."

*"'The servant came back and reported this to his master. Then
the owner of the house became angry and ordered his servant,
"Go out quickly into the streets and alleys of the town and
bring in the poor, the crippled, the blind and the lame."*

*""'Sir," the servant said, "what you ordered has
been done, but there is still room."*

*"'Then the master told his servant, "Go out to the roads and country
lanes and compel them to come in, so that my house will be full.""""*
-Luke 14:16-23

Beloved, there is urgency with the reality that Jesus will come back for us
one day soon and the fact there are many who haven't been invited to the
banquet. It is with urgency I write to you to build the house of the Lord
because all we bring to Heaven is people. But there are some the Lord is
tapping on the shoulder and asking if you'll shift your perspective from
building your kingdom to building His. It comes with invitation, vision,
hope, expectation, and wonder. He would only ask you to do this if there
was great reward and abundance ahead. Will you be one who picks up her
lamp and asks the Lord to fill it with the oil of His Spirit?

> Lord, shore up our resolve for You. Hem us in on every
> side, Jesus, and protect us from the evil one, who would
> love for us to be about our own lives and our own king-
> dom. I pray for this new wave of worship to crash over my
> sister, that she would be overcome with Your goodness and
> Your glory. I pray that the things entangling her would be
> untied so she can run with fervor and passion toward her

finish line, which is Christ Jesus. Lord, let her be part of the remnant—just like in Haggai—who hears the invitation of the Lord, stops everything, and turns toward Your voice. I bless my sister today with even deeper passion for You, Lord.

Listen to this worship song: "Holy Ground" by Passion

Day Fourteen

---❦---

His Glory is Coming

""But now be strong, Zerubbabel," declares the Lord. "Be strong, Joshua son of Jozadak, the high priest. Be strong, all you people of the land," declares the Lord, "and work. For I am with you," declares the Lord Almighty. "This is what I covenanted with you when you came out of Egypt. And my Spirit remains among you. Do not fear."

"'This is what the Lord Almighty says: "In a little while I will once more shake the heavens and the earth, the sea and the dry land. I will shake all nations, and what is desired by all nations will come, and I will fill this house with glory," says the Lord Almighty. "The silver is mine and the gold is mine," declares the Lord Almighty. "The glory of this present house will be greater than the glory of the former house," says the Lord Almighty. "And in this place I will grant peace," declares the Lord Almighty."
-Haggai 2:4-9

There was one month of silence between Haggai chapters 1 and 2, and the Lord came with His promise of glory. He needed some things set right in the hearts of His people. Babylon was being purified out of them. Their vision was being reset and realigned to the purposes of God. Their feet had to be set in motion. The people began to build the house of the Lord that was in ruins without knowing what was coming. And then God spoke, *"Be strong … work … Do not fear (Haggai 2:4-5)."* Action accompanied their hearing from the Lord. And a promise of blessing came and set vision before them as they worked.

Solomon's temple was glorious, but nothing compared to the glory of what was coming. We know that is Christ in us, the hope of glory. We became His temple—the place His Spirit and His glory dwells. Haggai was prophesying the glory of God filling the temple, but the desire of all nations is Jesus, and what He is doing in the Earth today is glorious through His people. It was a prophetic promise for then and now.

We have been made glory containers. We carry His glory, His purposes, His heart because He lives in us. And out of us flow living waters that touch the lives of those we engage with, here and all over the world. What a joyous calling and privilege. In our American culture of individualism, it's intimidating to share our lives and our stories and our Jesus with people. But if souls are going to be won for Jesus, we want to be right in the middle of it. I don't want to be on the bleachers cheering the harvest in; I want to have my "beautiful feet" in the field, working and praying alongside one another. Will you come with me?

The Bride is arising. I receive testimony after testimony of women whose hearts are coming alive. They are experiencing a revival of love for the One their hearts adore. The Holy Spirit is being poured out on sons and daughters, fueling courageous and passionate resolve. As you read these words, if this is the desire of your heart, will you say to the Lord, "I want this, Jesus. Will You do this in me? I surrender my life and plans and purposes to You today."

In 2004, I sat in Saddleback Church in California, where we were attending at the time. Rick Warren said, "I dare you to pray the most dangerous prayer of your life: 'God, send me.'" I remember distinctly thinking, "I have prayed that hundreds of times (I had just given birth to daughter number four) and He never answers, but here it goes." I think I got a wink from Heaven because months later, we received a clear call from the Lord to move to Texas, and the journey began.

A short time ago, I penned these words: "Do you think Jesus is getting His sandals back on?" It was pertaining to His long-awaited return. But right now, I have a sense the Holy Spirit is asking us the very same question:

Will you get your sandals back on?

Do not despise the days of preparation. He will restore all the years the locusts have eaten. You have been made ready for this time in history—to bear His glory. The harvest field needs your beautiful feet, your authority in ministry because of the places only you have walked; your hours of deep intercession for all God has called you to stand in the gap for; the tears you have sown; your voice of victorious worship; your glorious testimony that is covered in the blood of Jesus; your yes you have declared for all these years. Get ready for your yes to be answered. Long ago He put the longing in your heart to follow Him no matter where He takes you, and He will be faithful to answer it. I promise. I can testify to this truth.

So, glorious one, whose beautiful feet will bring Jesus His inheritance—the nations—it's time to get ready. Our greatest days are upon us. Throw off fear and intimidation from the spirit of darkness. There's a harvest field and a great number of women who need to be brought out of the shadows and sidelines.

> *"'Look at the nations and watch—and be utterly amazed.*
> *For I am going to do something in your days that you*
> *would not believe, even if you were told.'"*
> -Habakkuk 1:5

His House is being rebuilt right now; that's us. Everything is being shaken. Haggai and the writer of Hebrews 12:26-27 were on point. But it's not because He's angry; it's because of His passionate love for His Bride and the world. How He longs that no one misses Him and we carry the mandate of that commissioning. So, beloved sister, will you dare to pray this prayer?

"God, send me."

Let Him speak to you these 40-day journey, to reset your heart and your desires. Lay it all before Him—every fear and concern. His glory will come—absolutely it will. We just want to be the ones He sees as ready vessels, containers made ready for what is ahead.

Listen to this worship song: "Such an Awesome God" by Maverick City Music featuring Maryanne J. George

Day Fifteen

DON'T WORRY, HE HAS YOU

"'Therefore I tell you, do not be anxious about your life, what you will eat or what you will drink, nor about your body, what you will put on. Is not life more than food, and the body more than clothing? Look at the birds of the air: they neither sow nor reap nor gather into barns, and yet your heavenly Father feeds them. Are you not of more value than they? And which of you by being anxious can add a single hour to his span of life? And why are you anxious about clothing? Consider the lilies of the field, how they grow: they neither toil nor spin, yet I tell you, even Solomon in all his glory was not arrayed like one of these. But if God so clothes the grass of the field, which today is alive and tomorrow is thrown into the oven, will he not much more clothe you, O you of little faith? Therefore do not be anxious, saying, "What shall we eat?" or "What shall we drink?" or "What shall we wear?" For the Gentiles seek after all these things, and your heavenly Father knows that you need them all. But seek first the kingdom of God and his righteousness, and all these things will be added to you.'"
-Matthew 6:25-33, ESV

I had a profound moment one Sunday with a dear friend who was praying for breakthrough for me. During that time, the Lord showed me the picture of a sparrow in His hands. The vision lingers in this tumultuous season when the atmospheric winds are swirling. We are being kept and hidden and protected and provided for more than we realize. Not only that, but the abundance of Heaven is at our disposal.

In January 2020, I had the joy of taking a team of 18 women to Latin America. It was an incredibly large team, and I didn't quite understand why God had me taking so many women at once. Well, He knew the country where we visited was going to soon be closing, and He had prepared many to desire Him. Recently I heard from my translator that the people have endured much in this Latin American nation. She wrote these precious words, "As you said, the world has been shaken. We all have looked for new creative ways of being close to loved ones, of surviving, working, and healing. Thank God for His merciful provision of our daily bread. About church, it is closed again these days, but some sisters and my family gather at home to continue praying to keep our lamps full in case the Groom decides to come."

I sense a massive shift of perspective happening in Christians all over the world. God is awakening us to greater dependence on Him than we have known.

Jesus uses the illustration of the birds of the air—they have no concern or worry. They don't toil and spin and store up their treasures in large storehouses. In just a few verses before this passage, Jesus says,

> *"Do not lay up for yourselves treasures on earth, where moth and rust destroy and where thieves break in and steal, but lay up for yourselves treasures in heaven, where neither moth nor rust destroys and where thieves do not break in and steal. For where your treasure is, there your heart will be also."*
> -Matthew 6:19-21, ESV

Why would we store up our treasures on Earth in storehouses when God has treasures in Heaven stored up for us?

*"'Bring the whole tithe into the storehouse, that there may be food
in my house. Test me in this,' says the Lord Almighty, 'and see if
I will not throw open the floodgates of heaven and pour out so
much blessing that there will not be room enough to store it.'"*
-Malachi 3:10

As sons and daughters of the Most High God, we can trust Him for our
provision. I wish I could look those of you in the eyes who have lost jobs.
I would say to you: "You can trust Him for your provision." He has a
storehouse of provision, and the veil between Heaven and Earth has been
lifted. We worry and fret about our lives, and Jesus is inviting us to live
from Heaven's perspective. He's inviting us to live in full dependence on
Him. If Jesus has more than enough, will He not be gracious to you? Will
He not be abundantly good to you?

*"He who did not spare his own Son, but gave him up for us all—how
will he not also, along with him, graciously give us all things?"*
-Romans 8:32

He does not withhold Himself from us. If He doesn't withhold from the
flowers of the fields or the birds of the air, why would He withhold His
goodness from you?

It's a moment of divine invitation to begin to fill the storehouses of Heaven
with our treasures laid down on Earth. It's our time to live for Heaven, no
matter what Earth has to say. Your life is more than food or clothing or
storing up earthly wealth. Your life is more than temporal things that rust
and moths can destroy. You have eternal matters to engage your heart with
and to pursue. In fact, there is a dying and desperate world waiting for you
to shift your gaze from the temporal to the eternal. It's time to speak to
them and demonstrate to them the salvation and hope of Jesus. We don't
take anything to Heaven with us except people.

"Nevertheless, many Christians dread the thought of leaving this world. Why? Because so many have stored up their treasures on Earth, not in Heaven. Each day brings us closer to death. If your treasures are on Earth, each day brings you closer to losing them." -Randy Alcorn[7]

Sister, I have known nothing more urgent in my spirit than what God has been speaking to me for over a year. Jesus is returning, and it's time to get ready for that day. It's time to live from Heaven's perspective with our lamps filled with oil, dressed in royal robes of righteousness. His clothing for us is more glorious than anything we can purchase at Nordstrom. His food for us is a feast of goodness—manna from Heaven each day if we will just open our mouths to receive it. His storehouses of abundance are available to us. And daily there are treasures He puts before us to delight us with wonder and worship.

"Your identity is holiness unto the Lord. That is who you are. You are a saint of the Most High God. You are destined to wear a spotless and glorious gown for all of eternity. You have been set apart for the Bridegroom and for Him alone. You are His and He is yours. You are one with the Bridegroom. This is your identity. This is your calling. This is your inheritance. This is your destiny." -Christina McCracken[8]

Seek first His kingdom, and all these things will be added to you (Matthew 6:33). It's the order of our lives; it's who we are and what we do.

"This choice—to seek first the kingdom of God—is the fundamental choice everyone makes when they first repent and are converted. Yet every day after that, our Christian life will either reinforce that decision or deny it." -David Guzik, Matthew 6 commentary

Worry has no space in this reality because we know who we belong to and who has us in the palms of His nail-pierced hands. You belong to Him, your reigning King of victory and triumph.

> Lord, do a miraculous shift in the heart of my sister to live with eternity at the forefront of her life. Anoint her with faith that dissolves worry and anxiety. Lift her above the muck and the mire, the confusion and noise of the hour to come higher and hear what You have to say about it all. Protect her home and job and family and faith. Open over her the storehouses of Heaven and feed her like You do the birds of the air. May we be women who take You at Your word and trust You more than the temporal things of the world. Fortify us with faith and vision for what You are doing in the Earth and for the day very soon when we will see You face-to-face.

> *"Steep your life in God-reality, God-initiative, God-provisions. Don't worry about missing out. You'll find all your everyday human concerns will be met."*
> -Matthew 6:33, MSG

Listen to this worship song: "Sparrows" by Cory Asbury

COME AND JOIN ME

*"After the crowds dispersed, Jesus went up into the hills to
pray. And as night fell he was there praying alone.*

*"But the disciples, who were now in the middle of the lake, ran into
trouble, for their boat was tossed about by the high winds and heavy seas.*

*"At about four o'clock in the morning, Jesus came to them,
walking on the waves! When the disciples saw him walking on
top of the water, they were terrified and screamed, 'A ghost!'*

"Then Jesus said, 'Be brave and don't be afraid. I am here!'

*"Peter shouted out, 'Lord, if it's really you, then
have me join you on the water!'*

"'Come and join me,' Jesus replied.

*"So Peter stepped out onto the water and began to walk toward
Jesus. But when he realized how high the waves were, he became
frightened and started to sink. 'Save me, Lord!' he cried out.*

*"Jesus immediately stretched out his hand and lifted him up and
said, 'What little faith you have! Why would you let doubt win?'*

*"And the very moment they both stepped into
the boat, the raging wind ceased."*
-Matthew 14:23-32, TPT

The Lord woke me one morning with this story on my mind. I knew it was for us, so I stepped into the waters of this Scripture for a few days to pull out what the Holy Spirit would have us hear. For years I heard message after message on Peter's little faith in the middle of the storm, but what I sense that is even greater is the invitation of Jesus. It's our invitation—*"Come and join me.'"* In fact, there's so much to this story, I will share the second half in Day Seventeen.

Peter was the one and only one willing to step out and test the waters. Everyone else was paralyzed in fear, but if that 'ghost' could possibly be Jesus, that's who Peter wanted. Eleven had an encounter with fear, and one zealous and curious man longed for an encounter with Jesus. All in the middle of a storm, in the dark of night, when no one else would go with him, the invitation of his friend called out from the middle of the waves.

Peter longed for the impossible. He knew the laws of gravity. But this moment to walk with Jesus on impossibility defied all logical reason.

Peter wasn't thrown overboard like Jonah, in order to calm the raging sea. He also wasn't shipwrecked like Paul in order that an entire island would be saved. He was invited to come and supernaturally walk on the waters with Jesus. I wonder what he pictured the outcome to be. Did it cross his mind that he could possibly sink? Did he see himself jumping from one crest of the wave to another?

Peter longed for the impossible. He knew the laws of gravity. Gravity was at play in the natural because it's a force in the natural realm we live in. But this moment to walk with Jesus on impossibility defied all logical reason, and the supernatural became more real than the natural. When "natural" reasoning kicked in, Peter began to sink.

It was faith that kept Peter on the top of impossibility.

Peter had an opportunity to be offended at God in that moment. He could have said, "You invited me out here knowing I could sink; why would you even do that? Didn't you want to see my miracle all the way to the other side?" Jesus had much for Peter in that moment that would bear fruit for the rest of his life.

Before Jesus invited him into deep waters, He honored the curious faith in Peter and called him to come. Jesus' invitation on the shores back when He first called Peter to come and follow Him is the same invitation to a life of wonder and adventure. Jesus had more for Peter than he could imagine. Peter would be the one on the day of Pentecost to lead 3,000 Jews to the arms of Jesus. He would also be central to the Gentile Pentecost in Acts 10.

I presume Peter had a blank slate as it pertained to his experiential relationship with Jesus. His heart lived for these moments. He was beginning to believe God for impossible things. He wasn't bound by a Christian religious box or even expectations from past seasons. He just wanted to do what Jesus was doing. It was new, and it was wondrous. We can get so bound up intellectually or in fear that we never accept the invitation to the grand and glorious life with Christ that defies our rationale.

This is a season that is pregnant with invitation from Jesus. *"Come and join me ... ."* It's a pregnant pause for a divine reset and preparation, dear Bride of Christ.

Peter's life was anchored in radical faith—submitting caution to the wind of the Spirit. After his reinstatement on the beach with Jesus, post resurrection, he was literally unleashed. The Church was born on the shoulders of this young believer. Those shoulders that carried the shame of denying Jesus were the shoulders by which the church (Jew and Gentile) was born.

This is why he writes about refining faith in 1 Peter 1:6-7—he experienced this with the Lord. He entered the furnace of purification and came forth as gold. And Jesus stood by his side praying for him (Luke 22:32). The enemy wouldn't have the final word; there was a destiny over Peter's life, for the sake of the world, that would be fulfilled.

"Humble yourselves, therefore, under God's mighty hand, that he may lift you up in due time. Cast all of your anxiety on him because he cares for you."
-1 Peter 5:6-7

Peter experienced the humility of surrender and dependence on Jesus on this sea and many other "seas" of his life. He could say with confidence that Jesus will lift you up. He will protect you. He will not let you drown. When you are sinking and anxious, He will lift you up. He did it for me. He will do it for you. Again and again, over and over, without condemnation or hesitation.

From a fishing vessel to impacting the global Church, the Lord was faithful to fulfill His destiny over Peter's life that was given before the foundations of the world. Even an uneducated fisherman, filled with the spirit of God, can write a book or two that will be used to bring strength to the Church worldwide. (Some of you need to get writing that book you know the Lord is calling you to write!)

> Sister, Jesus is longing to defy logical reason in your life. All your self-talk of "I'm too old" or "I'm too afraid" or "I'm not gifted" aren't reasons; they are excuses. The mere invitation of Jesus was proof of the promise of the miracle. When Peter says, *"Lord, if it's really you (Matthew 14:28),"* it shows his uncertainty. All Peter needed to hop out of that

boat was one word, one invitation, to just hear His voice. Sister, we get to hear His voice. He speaks all the time. Don't allow anyone to tell you He doesn't speak to you. Don't let them snatch away the wonder of intimacy you can have with the Lord. We dine, dance, walk, worship, converse, adventure, and partner with a very intimate, loving, and communicative God. It's our inheritance as daughters to speak with the God who created the entire world. Oh, the majesty of such intimacy, and He's calling you to *"Come and join me (Matthew 14:29, TPT)"*.

Guard your heart against offense when trial comes or when you feel like you are sinking. God will lift you up in due time, and you will experience the supernatural power of God. Allow Him to deposit, deep within you, all you are to pull forth from these encounters with Him. Guard your heart, and trust Him with the process. He can handle the doubt along the way. And don't be offended with the ways of God when you don't understand them. After Kalley Heiligenthal (the artist of our worship song today) experienced the death of her baby girl, she stood with tender resolve to worship. She had a choice to remain with Jesus. He was faithful to lift her out of deep waters when she was drowning. She strengthens the melody of the Bride in worship.

I pray you will hear the voice of your Beloved calling you to come and join Him on the top of the water, regardless of whether it is still or tumultuous. Out of this encounter, faith will be refined, and you will have a testimony of extraordinary encounter and worship. Come and join Him; that's the safest place to be.

Listen to this worship song: "All That I'm After" by Kalley Heiligenthal

---

DO YOU HEAR HIS VOICE?

"'Lord, if it's you,' Peter replied, 'tell me to come to you on the water.'

"'Come,' he said.

"Then Peter got down out of the boat, walked on the water and came toward Jesus. But when he saw the wind, he was afraid and, beginning to sink, cried out, 'Lord, save me!'

"Immediately Jesus reached out his hand and caught him. 'You of little faith,' he said, 'why did you doubt?'

"And when they climbed into the boat, the wind died down. Then those who were in the boat worshiped him, saying, 'Truly you are the Son of God.'

"When they had crossed over, they landed at Gennesaret. And when the men of that place recognized Jesus, they sent word to all the surrounding country. People brought all their sick to him and begged him to let the sick just touch the edge of his cloak, and all who touched it were healed."
-Matthew 14:28-36

A few years ago, we met our dear friends, the Gloudes, in Breckenridge, Colorado. We decided to go white water rafting one afternoon. Half of us piled into one raft, and Mike and I and two of our girls got in the second raft. As we were maneuvering our way down the rapids, the Lord began to speak to me about the rafting guide on our boat. He asked me to pray for this man's wife to get pregnant. I began analyzing what God was saying with objections like, "I don't even know if he's married; he's going to think I'm strange. How and when do I do this?" Suddenly, our raft hit an enormously large, submerged rock and, lo and behold, I went flying into the water. To sum up the next five minutes, I was literally in over my head, trying to hold onto my sunglasses, trying not to drown, and trying to hear the direction of the guide yelling, "Swim!" The raft caught up to me, and the weight of the raft kept my head below water. I found myself trapped beneath with absolutely no way out. Then my husband leaned over the front of the raft and somehow found me and pulled me to the side and up into the raft.

After gasping for air, I looked at the guide who said, "I haven't had someone thrown overboard in 10 years!" I said to him, "That's because God wants me to pray for your wife to get pregnant, and I was finding every reason not to." With wide eyes, he looked at me and said, "My wife has not been able to get pregnant, and we've been trying for a very long time." Once we got to shore, I prayed and prophesied over that man and his wife, finding out that his mom was a believer and had prayed for him to come back to Jesus for many, many years. That divine appointment on that day needed my obedience, and God had equally as much for me as for that guide.

When Peter heard the voice of Jesus in the midst of blowing winds and crashing waves, the familiarity of the tone of his invitation captured Peter's attention—His precious, familiar voice. Peter needed His voice while in the boat or on the waves. As they got back in the boat, the storm ceased, and worship began.

Getting back in the boat with Jesus is just as important as launching out in faith. You need your place of refuge with Him and with others. Joining the faith of others in the place of worship, as the 12 did together, is a necessity in stormy waters. Hungry people invite the presence of God, and He comes with fire and fullness, peace, and stillness. The storm doesn't define the character of God but rather redefines His goodness, power, and presence. Faith is born in opposition and trial because God always comes through.

Worship is the highway to faith!

"Now faith brings our hopes into reality and becomes the foundation needed to acquire the things we long for. It is all the evidence required to prove what is still unseen. This testimony of faith is what previous generations were commended for. Faith empowers us to see that the universe was created and beautifully coordinated by the power of God's words! He spoke and the invisible realm gave birth to all that is seen."
-Hebrews 11:1-3, TPT

Sister, fan into flame this faith the Holy Spirit has supplied you to believe Him for who He is. He's faithful to fulfill the destiny over your life. But this requires your partnership. Walking on water isn't a passive, observant position; it's a radical, faith-filled partnership. He will stir up the wind of His Spirit beneath you so you can soar. He is inviting you to *"'Come'"* and walk on impossibility. He will supply the supernatural faith, the supernatural encounter, the supernatural rescue. He will bring His overwhelming presence that causes you to fall face down in worship. This storm right now in America is an opportunity to refine and restore your faith and take you deeper into supernatural encounter as you cross over.

Please hear me. This tumultuous season of perceived setback is a divine appointment for a reset for faith. There are destinies over your life, the Church, and this nation God wants to see fulfilled. But He wants our intercession, faith, worship, and partnership to bring them forth. It's not a time for passivity and lucid observation. It's a time to press in, repent, intercede and move as He invites you to *"'Come'"* into deeper intimacy. It's out of these moments with Jesus that Peter could pen the words:

"But these only reveal the sterling core of your faith, which is far more valuable than gold that perishes, for even gold is refined by fire. Your authentic faith will result in even more praise, glory, and honor when Jesus the Anointed One is revealed."
-1 Peter 1:7, TPT

I have a precious friend, Elizabeth, who is undergoing chemotherapy. The Lord awakened her in the middle of the night and placed these words in her spirit: Elizabeth, worship Me. She began to do just that, and His presence came, and her spirit was strengthened. He came and overwhelmed her with His goodness.

It's important to notice what is on the other side of this encounter for Jesus, Peter, and the other 11 disciples. Remember that when there is a battle or a trial, we must know that breakthrough is coming. There was a whole town (and surrounding country) awaiting an encounter with Jesus.

"After they crossed over and landed at Gennesaret, the people living there quickly recognized who he was. They were quick to spread the news throughout the surrounding region that Jesus had come to them. So they brought him all their sick, begging him to let them touch the fringe of his cloak. And everyone who touched it was instantly healed!"
-Matthew 14:34-36, TPT

This miraculous moment of watching Jesus heal so many people was deeply deposited in Peter's life. Not only did he have this memory, but he also later housed the Holy Spirit inside of him, so when he met the crippled beggar at the gate beautiful, he knew exactly what to offer him.

> *"Then Peter said, 'I don't have money, but I'll give you this—by the power of the name of Jesus Christ of Nazareth, stand up and walk!' Peter held out his right hand to the crippled man. As he pulled the man to his feet, suddenly power surged into his crippled feet and ankles. The man jumped up, stood there for a moment stunned, and then began to walk around! As he went into the temple courts with Peter and John, he leapt for joy and shouted praises to God."*
> -Acts 3:6-8, TPT

Beloved sister, we must hear His voice above all other voices. Tuck into Him because He has so much He wants to show you, and He's calling you to *"Come."* Walking on waves with Jesus; worshipping in the storm; watching Jesus heal people who merely touched His cloak are just the beginning for you—just as it was for Peter. He has even more for you in the coming days.

I want to prophesy this truth to you: The current global storm is not the end of the story. It's an opportunity for a profound encounter to come fully alive into the purposes of God in this moment in history. It's an opportunity to bring a whole village, city, or country the healing power of Jesus. It's a time to walk on impossibility and move Heaven and Earth in prayer to see the purposes of God fulfilled in our lifetime. It's time to speed His return and bring in a massive harvest of souls. This is your time, your invitation to awaken and arise. Jesus is coming for His Bride, who is full of faith and zeal for the One her heart longs for! Just ask Him to do this in you. He will birth things through your life you could only read in the chronicles written in Heaven. Get ready. Get positioned. It's coming.

Listen to this worship song: "Know Your Heart" by David Leonard

Day Eighteen

---✙---

A WEAPON FORGED IN FIRE

"Then Nebuchadnezzar was furious with Shadrach, Meshach and Abednego, and his attitude toward them changed. He ordered the furnace heated seven times hotter than usual and commanded some of the strongest soldiers in his army to tie up Shadrach, Meshach and Abednego and throw them into the blazing furnace. So these men, wearing their robes, trousers, turbans and other clothes, were bound and thrown into the blazing furnace. The king's command was so urgent and the furnace so hot that the flames of the fire killed the soldiers who took up Shadrach, Meshach and Abednego, and these three men, firmly tied, fell into the blazing furnace."
-Daniel 3:19-23

Mighty weapons are being forged right now in the fire of refinement.

In fact, these aren't just ordinary weapons; these ones are being fashioned in the hand of God, with the very breath of God. They will demolish strongholds of every kind. They will set captives free. They will be crafted in the secret place with Jesus. They will carry the plans of Heaven to be released on the Earth with a new song in their mouths and their hands trained for battle. It may feel seven times hotter, but seven is a biblical number of completion. With all my heart, I believe Jesus is finishing what He began in you.

Three young men, Shadrach, Meshach, and Abednego were positioned front and center in the culture of Babylon, a culture of self-indulgence, secularism, and self-worship. These men chose again and again not to be defiled but to remain outside of what would not be popular by the vast majority. With every test came a more resolute conviction to be set apart. Then came the ultimate test: the fiery furnace. With all eyes on them, they determined they would not bow to the king's idol. They would not bend a knee to anything or anyone other than God Himself. And before they were bound and thrown, they declared to the king,

"'King Nebuchadnezzar, we do not need to defend ourselves before you in this matter. If we are thrown into the blazing furnace, the God we serve is able to deliver us from it, and he will deliver us from Your Majesty's hand. But even if he does not, we want you to know, Your Majesty, that we will not serve your gods or worship the image of gold you have set up.'"
-Daniel 3:16-18

Jesus came and stood with them, like He always does. He showed up in the middle of the fire.

Nebuchadnezzar acknowledged this when he said,

"'Look! I see four men walking around in the fire, unbound and unharmed, and the fourth looks like a son of the gods."
-Daniel 3:25

Jesus stood right in the middle of the fire as these three weapons, cupped in the hand of the Most High God, were being forged. Two glorious moments in this story: when Jesus came to encounter these three guys and how they left the trial unbound and unharmed, not even smelling like smoke.

"They saw that the fire had not harmed their bodies, nor
was a hair of their heads singed; their robes were not
scorched, and there was no smell of fire on them."
-Daniel 3:27

Our guys aren't mentioned in the book of Daniel after this moment. But Jesus never stops showing up again and again through every story of Scripture, with His presence and power moving from before creation through all of eternity. He brings deliverance and victory and redemption to every believer of Christ and to every act of the enemy, who tries to steal, kill, and destroy the people of God.

I need you to hear these words: If God is for you, who can be against you (Romans 8:31)?

The Bride is being forged in the fire of purity and refinement, and she will come forth as gold. She will not smell like smoke nor will her gown be singed. She will come forth radiant, purified, and ablaze with the glory of God.

"'See, I am the one who created the craftsman who fans the coals
into a fire and forges a weapon fit for its purpose, and I am the one
who created the destroyer to destroy. But I promise you, no weapon
meant to hurt you will succeed, and you will refute every accusing
word spoken against you. This promise is the inheritance of Yahweh's
servants, and their vindication is from me,' says Yahweh."
-Isaiah 54:16-17, TPT

I would like to interject a new idea as it pertains to this Scripture in Isaiah and our three fearless guys in Daniel. I have researched and researched whether the blacksmith and the destroyer are the same person. Nothing I have read confirms this connection, which leads me to this conclusion: God uses anything to make us a weapon in His hand, fit for His purposes.

If we read Scripture through the lens of spiritual warfare and we know we have been commissioned to invade the kingdom of darkness and storm the gates of Hell, don't you think we would be fashioned to not only carry the sword of the Spirit but to be a sword in this hour by the power of His Spirit? Perhaps in a counter move of what the enemy is forging for our demise, God is forging a weapon in us for the victory, deliverance, and redemption of families, cities, and nations. I would like to think that as much as Paul told Timothy to *"fan into flame the gift of God (2 Timothy 1:6)"* that God is breathing His breath on the coals of our lives to bring forth something glorious for His name's sake that has victory written all over it.

There are certain things that can only come forth through fire for the people of God—to be made like gold and to be made into a weapon to partner with God's purposes. Both are precious to the Lord. When the hand of God brings you through a fire, you better believe it's for ultimate redemption and victory. What weapon would God forge that wouldn't be destined for victory? What person who is purified and comes forth as gold would not have the costliest testimony of redemption? This was Job's testimony after all his trials by fire.

> *"But He knows the way that I take [and He pays attention to it]. When He has tried me, I will come forth as [refined] gold [pure and luminous]."*
> -Job 23:10, AMP

Not one ounce of what you have endured will be wasted. Not one tear that has fallen in any season—past, present, or future—will fall unredeemed. There is nothing that withholds the victory of Jesus, in the life of a believer surrendered to His purposes. You are coming forth as gold, dear sister. Everything that needs to be purified and made spotless will be made so on the basis of love. And as much as you smell the smoke of fiery trials, your fragrance will not be smoke. You will come through with a testimony of His goodness and power that will be celebrated for all of eternity. Jesus puts His name on our trials because He places His name on us. Our conquering

King puts His banner over us, His banner of love. He writes "overcomer," "victorious," and "free" on you.

> "Harvest is coming. A mighty outpouring is coming, but *first* the cleansing must come. The Lord is already moving, revival fires are burning in different places, the Spirit of God is beginning to move, but this is a very somber moment in the body of Christ right now. The degree to which we embrace the cleansing and purging upon the Church will be the degree to which we run with Him in what He is going to do in the earth. That is not the Lord dictating who will run with Him and who won't; He wants all to run with Him. It's dependent upon how much we embrace the fire of cleansing and purification that He is bringing. Embracing the purging, embracing His fire and His correction brings us deeper into intimacy with Jesus. It's a personal revival that's upon those who embrace what He is doing to cause a deeper yielding and devotion to Jesus. To be all consumed, overcome, and in love with Him at a level never walked in before." -Lana Vawser[9]

Lord, I pray that both perspective and hope come forth in the spirit of my sister. You are doing something miraculous in this furnace that's been turned up to seven times hotter. You will finish what You have begun in her life; this is what You promised. So, anchor her in those times she finds herself in the fiery furnace, in the greatest encounter of love she has ever known. Purify us, Your Bride, to be ready and dressed for the coming days. Make us weapons for Your purposes, Jesus, as we partner with You in this new era. I pray we would carry new gifts of healing and deliverance. I pray we would walk about in joy and excitement because these are the most exciting days to be alive in all of history. Sustain us by Your goodness and abundance, in Jesus' name!

Listen to this worship song: "Another in the Fire" by Hillsong UNITED

Day Nineteen

---✦---

BREAKTHROUGH ANOINTING | MANY STRATEGIES, ONE VICTORY

"David then took up residence in the fortress and called it the City of David. He built up the area around it, from the terraces inward. And he became more and more powerful, because the Lord God Almighty was with him. ...

"When the Philistines heard that David had been anointed king over Israel, they went up in full force to search for him, but David heard about it and went down to the stronghold. Now the Philistines had come and spread out in the Valley of Rephaim; so David inquired of the Lord, 'Shall I go and attack the Philistines? Will you deliver them into my hands?'

"The Lord answered him, 'Go, for I will surely deliver the Philistines into your hands.'

"So David went to Baal Perazim, and there he defeated them. He said, 'As waters break out, the Lord has broken out against my enemies before me.' So that place was called Baal Perazim. The Philistines abandoned their idols there, and David and his men carried them off.

"Once more the Philistines came up and spread out in the Valley of Rephaim; so David inquired of the Lord, and he answered, 'Do not go straight up, but circle around behind them and attack

them in front of the poplar trees. As soon as you hear the sound
of marching in the tops of the poplar trees, move quickly, because
that will mean the Lord has gone out in front of you to strike the
Philistine army.' So David did as the Lord commanded him, and he
struck down the Philistines all the way from Gibeon to Gezer."
-2 Samuel 5:9-10, 17-25

We find David, at just age 30, crowned with the title and responsibility of king. He had walked through 15 years of preparation with the Lord to be made ready for his day of leadership and battle. In today's Scripture, David faced his enemies. With increased anointing, the power of God was manifest through his life for breakthrough for the people of God. Greatness and victory were not born in one day; they were deposited in David in the years of preparation before this moment. God knew the task before David as well as the battles he would face, so the preparation was mandatory. Oh, the kindness and love of God.

I beseech you: Do not despise your days of preparation.

> "In God's plan there is almost always a hidden price of greatness. Often those who become great among God's people experience much pain and difficulty in God's training process." -David Guzik, 2 Samuel 5 commentary

As David sought the Lord, he had success. He was able to partner with God to bring victory to His people, Israel. It was like waters broke forth that could not be contained. The Lord honored David's dependence and his heart to seek Him first. In the first battle in this passage of Scripture, David defeated the Philistines with overwhelming force, carrying away the idols they brought to the battle. Nothing could stop or contain the power of God for victory. There was a breakthrough anointing on David for victory because he sought the Lord. And the Lord gave a word: Go!

"Before this breakthrough happened for David and Israel, the scene in Scripture is called the Valley of Rephaim, meaning 'house of the giant.' But here is what is awesome: After the breakthrough, it is called Ba'al Perazim, meaning 'Possessor of Breaches, Lord of the Breakthrough.' ... God broke through the stronghold of the enemy! He named his God above all the little giants of Baal. This still happens for us today. God breaks through in awesome ways that belittle our enemies and cause the oppression to look small in comparison to His strength." -Shawn Bolz[10]

A second battle emerged in the valley of Rephaim, and, once again, David sought the Lord for the strategy. This one would be different from the first; there would be a sign first for him to move. He didn't go out to fight based on the strategy of the last battle, even though this place had encountered the breakthrough power of God. Once again, he took his directives from the Lord. *"You shall not go up; circle around behind them (2 Samuel 5:23, NKJV)."* God gave David different directions for this battle. Even though the enemy was the same, not every battle is fought the same way. Then the Lord said to him, *"As soon as you hear the sound of marching in the tops of the poplar trees, move quickly ... (2 Samuel 5:24)."* This required David to wait for the Lord to strike the camp of the enemy first. As soon as David heard the sound of marching in the tops of the mulberry trees, he was to move.

God is gracious to say when we are to move and when we are to wait till He gives a sign. What is required of us is to inquire of Him before we do anything.

Sister, we carry the anointing of the Spirit of God for breakthrough and victory. He has not left us unarmed or without the ability to hear Him or respond to Him with the faith and power He supplies. Our very intimate relationship with the Father, Son, and Spirit enables us to face the enemy with confidence that the victory is ours. God desires to partner with us in everything to enforce the victory He paid for on the cross. It's our inheritance to plunder the camp of the enemy and enforce the kingdom of God here on Earth.

> "I can't afford to live in reaction to darkness. If I do, darkness has had a role in setting the agenda for my life. The devil is not worthy of such influence, even in the negative. Jesus lived in response to the Father. I must learn to do the same." -Bill Johnson[11]

God will give you clear direction for breakthrough and for overcoming your enemy. *"The horse is made ready for the day of battle, but victory rests with the Lord (Proverbs 21:31)."* He has been preparing you all these years to teach your hands to war. The trials and suffering, pain and perseverance have been a deposit into your life for these days. You also have been given a greater authority to minister out of the places of personal victory. Nothing is wasted. Everything matters for this day right now.

The Lord gave me a dream where women were gathered on their knees in desperation. I could sense a deeper level of surrender and longing. I knew I was to pray for an even greater anointing to fall on them. Many were on their knees and in tears. I too got on my knees to pray for them, and immediately I saw the image of feet come and stand in front of me. I knew in my dream they were God's feet. I began to weep in the presence of the Lord in my dream. And from that place, I prayed for the women. It was as though the Lord confirmed He was standing with me and would be answering their cries of surrender and worship and longing in preparation for the days to come. It was a holy dream of promise and vision to my spirit in where the Lord longs to take His women. He is making His Bride ready.

Every victory has its birthplace in dependence and surrender.

We are victors, period. But the strategy to victory will be different for each battle. This is why our lives have to be anchored in Jesus and completely wrapped in intimacy. We must know the heart of God before we take a step. We move when He says, *"Go."* But we don't move until He says to go. The days in which we are living require deep intimacy and worship, and His strategies will always lead to victory for His people. He is fighting for you; you need only be still and reside in this place of intimacy. He is for you. You are His, and His banner of victory is over you.

I want to pray for a Baal Perazim anointing for you—a breakthrough anointing born out of even deeper intimacy and authority in Christ Jesus. Many people have seen their camps plundered by the enemy, which was never God's heart. It's time to take back what the enemy has taken, that God may restore the years the locusts have eaten. You have been made ready for this day.

> Lord Jesus, thank You for Your invitation to even deeper surrender, worship, and victory. Thank You for increased authority and anointing to hear Your voice and to know the strategies of Heaven in this hour. Bring us to our knees in wondrous dependence and worship. Come today and stand before each woman. May she even have a picture of Your feet standing before her, ready to anoint her head with oil as You call her into this critical hour. Where the enemy has played his hand, raise up a standard against him. I pray for victory in the places where each woman has been waiting for victory, that You would grant her a break-through anointing accompanied by Heaven's strategies.
>
> Lord, increase her worship so that the enemy flees. Strengthen her innermost being to be steadfast and im-movable. Fix her eyes on You, Jesus. I pray against all fear in this hour—fear must go, in Jesus' name. She is seated in

heavenly places and operates with the mind of Christ, so let her pray and listen and move from this position. Pour out Your Spirit on my sisters today, and let them carry the fire of God in and through their laid down lives of surrender and worship. In Jesus' name, amen.

"A new song for a new day rises up in me every time I think about how he breaks through for me! Ecstatic praise pours out of my mouth until everyone hears how God has set me free. Many will see his miracles; they'll stand in awe of God and fall in love with him!"
-Psalm 40:3, TPT

Listen to this worship song: "Anything is Possible" by Bethel Music and Dante Bowe

Day   Twenty

ANCHORS DOWN

"Go ahead and give God thanks for all the glorious things he has done! Go ahead and worship him! Tell everyone about his wonders! Let's sing his praises! Sing, and put all of his miracles to music! Shine and make your joyful boast in him, you lovers of God. Let's be happy and keep rejoicing no matter what. Seek more of his strength! Seek more of him! Let's always be seeking the light of his face. Don't you ever forget his miracles and marvels. Hold to your heart every judgment he has decreed. For you are his servants, the true seed of Abraham, and you are the chosen ones, Jacob's sons. For he is the Lord our God, and his wise authority can be seen in all he does. For though a thousand generations may pass away, he is still true to his word. He has kept every promise he made to Abraham and to Isaac."
-Psalm 105:1-9, TPT

Oh, the great, great love of God. In a world that is seemingly spinning out of control, I think we need to hear that the radical and pursuing love of God never ceases. We are anchored in it. It's a banner over our heads. It knows no heights or depths or limits. In fact the love of God is so great, He went to unfathomable lengths of unlimited sacrifice to make sure we understood it. He withheld nothing and gave everything. His love conquers all.

Last summer, while visiting my brother in Alaska, I found myself completely overwhelmed in how much the Lord loves His creation. If my heart delights in the majesty and wonder of creation, how much more does God's heart delight in all He has created. We watched the sea otters carry their babies on their stomachs as they glided through the water. Glaciers and volcanoes, moose, bear, and whales declare the majestic wonder of God. There are birds of many colors; eagles who soar overhead as cliff swallows make their nests in the side of the rock faces. I thought, "If You care and delight in Your creation like this, how much greater do You love and care and delight in us?" The Holy Spirit placed these sweet words in my heart:

> If you could only grasp the depth of love I have for all I created!

I was overwhelmed and tearful because I don't think I really understand the depth of that truth.

> *"For God so loved the world that He gave his one and only Son, that whoever believes in him shall not perish but have eternal life."*
> -John 3:16

He loves the world without hesitation, and He doesn't want anyone to perish without knowing Him and encountering this radical and unexplainable love. So He goes out of His way to move Heaven and Earth to let us know.

When we don't understand the complexity of chaos or the spiritual forces of darkness at work, there is one thing we must let down and anchor ourselves in, and that is the love of God.

> *"Go ahead and give God thanks for all the glorious things he has done! Go ahead and worship him! Tell everyone about his wonders! Let's sing his praises!"*
> - Psalm 105:1-2a, TPT

He's worthy of our praise. He's worthy of our acknowledgment in the greatness of who He is. If we try and anchor in anything other than Jesus, we will drift.

When we went fishing in Alaska, there was a part of the ocean where two currents were converging in opposite directions. It was the best place to catch salmon, so we let down our anchor and cast our lines. Had we not anchored our boat in that spot of current convergence, we would have drifted in the chaos of the waters.

Let us anchor down so we can cast our lines and fish for people. The harvest field needs us anchored and overflowing in His love, being conduits of this great and glorious love of God. A dying world is waiting for an encounter with our living and loving God, who lives inside us. More than 3 billion people have yet to hear His name. Get your anchors down, and let's go fishing.

> Read Ephesians 3:14-21. Ask God to give you the same
> love He has for the world.

Listen to this worship song: "God is Love" by Chris Renzema

LOVE OVERFLOW

"And I pray that he would unveil within you the unlimited riches of his glory and favor until supernatural strength floods your innermost being with his divine might and explosive power.

"Then, by constantly using your faith, the life of Christ will be released deep inside you, and the resting place of his love will become the very source and root of your life.

"Then you will be empowered to discover what every holy one experiences—the great magnitude of the astonishing love of Christ in all its dimensions. How deeply intimate and far-reaching is his love! How enduring and inclusive it is! Endless love beyond measurement that transcends our understanding—this extravagant love pours into you until you are filled to overflowing with the fullness of God!

"Never doubt God's mighty power to work in you and accomplish all this. He will achieve infinitely more than your greatest request, your most unbelievable dream, and exceed your wildest imagination! He will outdo them all, for his miraculous power constantly energizes you.

"Now we offer up to God all the glorious praise that rises from every church in every generation through Jesus Christ—and all that will yet be manifest through time and eternity. Amen!"
-Ephesians 3:16-21, TPT

We are in an hour where the revelation of the love of God is not only transforming us at deeper and deeper levels but is moving the Bride of Christ to go into the harvest field where Jesus is inviting her. When we discover the overwhelming and unconditional love of God and we let it overtake us, the magnitude and depth of that love begins to overflow out of us. It flows to the highways and the byways in search of those who have no hope. It walks across states and streets to bring encounter to the desperate and dying. In these months of intensity, fear, chaos, and division, we must drop our anchors in the deep, deep love of Christ and draw close to His heart. Revival is propelled by love. Our nation and the nations of the world will see revival, in Jesus' name.

> "Revivalists burn with the urgency of the hour. Revival is not just simply an event or series of extended meetings; revival is a lifestyle. … God wants to use you as a catalyst for an earth-shaking, heaven-sent, move of the Holy Spirit in your life and in this nation. Are you ready?" -Jeremiah Johnson

In the fall of 2020, I had the joy of taking 24 women to Austin, Texas, to enjoy His presence and go into the harvest field to share the hope and good news of Jesus. I can honestly say, having ministered in the Middle East, the ground was as hard in Austin as it is in Muslim countries. It must be those same deceiving spirits that don't know geographical boundaries. We had one young woman instruct our team to "get away" simply because they exuded the presence of God. The opposition and rejection were alarming. Others we encountered had been searching, and God miraculously allowed us to intersect. We encountered believers sitting alone who, as soon as we asked them how we could pray for them, burst into tears. There were many opportunities to minister to discouraged and lonely Christ followers. We saw eight people give their lives to Jesus, which is the greatest miracle of all.

Beloved, it is time to drop our anchors into the extravagant love of God. It's this love that drives away all fear. It's this love that compels us to share the good news of Jesus even if we are mocked or criticized. People are getting desperate, and there's only one solution: Jesus. He's the answer for our nation, and as I have been praying for revival for decades, I believe we are nearing an end-time harvest like no one has ever seen. It's time to break our holy huddles and go.

> "Do not take His words lightly. They are your life. They are your daily bread. They are the place of protection for your heart and mind. The shaking upon the Church in this new era is to bring the eyes of the church away from 'look at me and my platform' and other loves and affections of the heart, back to the gaze of Jesus, eyes locked with Him. The dance of the first love. The place of humility where a life is laid down for one thing alone— Jesus Christ. I am not here to serve myself; I am not here to get glory for me and my name. I am here to make His name great. The one thing I want to be known for when I leave this earth is how my life was used to bring glory to Him, how His name was glorified and lifted high in and through my life, so that I would be known as one who loved God with all my heart, all my soul, all my mind." -Lana Vawser[12]

My heavenly download for the movement of Arise is seeing women called from the sidelines, connected to one another, and commissioned to the expansion of the kingdom of God across the Earth. Their eyes are fixed on Jesus, their lamps are full of oil, and worship is their weapon. They have thrown off the things that have entangled them in past seasons or even for generations, and Jesus has become the focus of their lives.

Even as the enemy uses his weapon of fear against the Bride, she is resolute and so anchored in the love of God that she is immovable.

A few months ago, the Lord took me to Numbers 11:16-17 and gave me the vision for 70 cities, 70 leaders who will call and connect women to a passionate pursuit of Jesus and a partnership with the Holy Spirit for the sake of the gospel. Will you pray with me for these 70 leaders? Will you ask the Lord what His heart is for your city and your sisters in Christ who live there? The Lord is doing something marvelous with women in this hour that is undeniably His heart as we see in the Gospels. Women have been sidelined long enough, and it's not OK with Jesus. He paid for their freedom and is commissioning them in this hour to be revivalists who walk in the revelation of His love.

So, with that reality, I want to bless you today with this Scripture from Ephesians.

> I pray that the words of God would transform your heart
> and mind. In the name of Jesus, I bless you with a strength
> and power in your innermost being. I bless you with the
> gift of faith, to believe God for impossibility, to hold onto
> every word that is yours in Scripture. I bless you with faith
> to pray beyond what your eyes have seen. I bless you to
> be anchored in the love of Jesus that keeps you steadfast
> and immovable. I bless you, in Jesus' name, with a fresh
> revelation of His love that literally transforms your mind,
> your vision, and your trajectory. I bless you today with the
> boundless reality of His love for you—the depth, width,
> height, and length that knows no limitation. I bless you to
> know in your mind, your soul, and your spirit the reviving

love of Jesus. As He fills everything in every way, I bless you to overflow in His love. May it be not a trickling river flowing out of you but whitewater rapids flowing out of your very life, that people would jump into your overflow and find the extraordinary love and grace of God. I bless you with the fire of His presence and a sanctified imagination to pray in immeasurably more than you can even dream or articulate. I bless you with a mouth to declare His praises and a life to carry His glory for all your days. In His matchless name, amen.

Listen to this worship song: "The More I Seek You" by Hannah McClure

Day Twenty-Two

---✦---

SHINE, DAUGHTERS OF GOD

"Those who are wise will shine like the brightness of the heavens, and those who lead many to righteousness, like the stars for ever and ever."
-Daniel 12:3

Daniel 12 is a prophetic account of the last days that coincides with Matthew 24. But set in verse 3 is this glorious vision and invitation for His Bride. God's people, like stars, are radiating light into a very dark world. They are the ones who help people find their way in darkness. Out of the overflow of their hearts their mouths speak wisdom and hope to a dying and desperate world. We are perfectly suited for this time in history, those of you positioned in worship and surrender. Your light will shine in darkness.

I was taken back to Genesis to read the account of when God created the stars:

"Then God said, 'Let there be light-bearers (sun, moon, stars) in the expanse of the heavens to separate the day from the night, and let them be useful for signs (tokens) [of God's provident care], and for marking seasons, days, and years; and let them be useful as lights in the expanse of the heavens to provide light on the earth'; and it was so, [just as He commanded]. God made the two great lights—the greater light (the sun) to rule the day, and the lesser light (the moon) to rule the night; He made

the [galaxies of] stars also [that is, all the amazing wonders in the heavens].
God placed them in the expanse of the heavens to provide light upon the
earth, to rule over the day and the night, and to separate the light from the
darkness; and God saw that it was good and He affirmed and sustained
it. And there was evening and there was morning, a fourth day."
-Genesis 1:14-19, AMP

There was a purpose in the breath of God creating the stars—it wasn't just to fill space and make the sky sparkly. They became signs for God's people for the first coming of Jesus and signs of times to come (like in Joel 3:14-16) before Jesus returns. Interesting to find God's invitation wrapped in the words of Daniel to the Bride who was yet to be born. But the description in Genesis is also quite parallel to our calling here on Earth: providing light upon the Earth, ruling over and separating darkness from light, and only sustained by God Himself! But according to Daniel 12:3, this also has an eternal purpose and significance.

National Geographic[13] states that "Stars are huge celestial bodies made mostly of hydrogen and helium that produce light and heat from the churning nuclear forges inside their cores. … They are the building blocks of galaxies, of which there are billions in the universe. It's impossible to know how many stars exist, but astronomers estimate that in our Milky Way galaxy alone, there are about 300 billion."

We are the building blocks of nations, societies, families, gospel movements, and the kingdom of God. (And remember, 3.2 billion people have yet to hear the name Jesus.) Within each believer is our churning nuclear center—Christ in us, the hope of glory! Out of our lives of worship and surrender comes this pulsating light and heat of His presence and His glory for all to see. In fact, we are invited to speak wisdom and live in a way that leads many to righteousness. The promise in Daniel 12 is for eternity; it's not a short-lived spotlight here on Earth. This promise won't fade or grow dim. It endures, and we get to invest our lives in the very thing that will last forever and ever!

So what does this invitation practically look like for us as the King's daughters, who are learning to walk as daughters, live out of a passion for Jesus, and carry His heart for the world?

It looks like women who have come alive and are living out of this place of worship and surrender for the One who held nothing back. It looks like a daughter who knows the love letter written for her, not on tablets of stone but on her human heart. It looks like out of the overflow of her heart, her mouth speaks wisdom and brings life to directionless, hopeless, and hurting people. She knows how to walk because she follows the nail-pierced feet in front of her. He is her guide, and the light that lives in her gives a path to those who follow her. Her lamp is filled with oil, and she's looking for other women who don't have their lamps yet filled. She will be distinguished in this culture of darkness, spoken of before the great cloud of witnesses, and honored for all eternity. She is breaking loose and shaking off the things that entangle her and keep her from running whole heartedly after the One her heart longs for.

The passions of the world are growing dim, and intimacy and the fire of passion in her bones for Jesus are increasing. She is wise in spiritual things, instructed in the Word, and sees the crowds with the same compassion Jesus had. When Scripture says *"He was moved with compassion (Matthew 9:36, AMP)"* when he saw the people, she too lives from Heaven's perspective. Her leadership will require faith-filled, risk-taking movement. She's arising in this hour with the declaration written across her life: *"For to me, to live is Christ … (Philippians 1:21)."*

It's not a passive thing to lead many to righteousness. It's intended to be a characteristic of every Christ follower. I pray that even as you read these words, you long for this overflow from your life. Will you live as one who's pulsating light attracts scores of people to Christ in you? Perhaps you are sick or stuck inside, and you feel limited to leading. Let me remind you of the power of a praying woman—she moves nations and brings prodigals home. The harvest is contingent on women who will pray this in now.

Remember the Samaritan woman who came to get water and encountered Jesus in the middle of the day? She ran back, and her whole village heard about Jesus. Remember Lydia, the first convert of Europe who started a church out of her home in Philippi? The lives of those in that church, consumed by Jesus, lead others to encounter Him and therefore brought forth great impact in the lives of others that reached villages and regions!

> "Now, Daniel's vision promises that the faithful shall shine like those stars—beautiful—dependable—useful—eternal. People would admire them. They would learn to guide by the light of their faithful mentors. Faithful people would bless all those who observed their lives, just as we are all blessed by the lights that God has placed in the sky. Surely with this verse in mind, Jesus concluded his Parable of the Weeds by saying: 'Then the righteous will shine forth like the sun in the kingdom of their Father' (Matthew 13:43)." -Richard Niell Donovan[14]

These are days where we need the wisdom of Scripture and the words of the Holy Spirit deeply deposited inside us. We must know the path we are to walk in these days of accelerated darkness. The Lord is looking for His Bride to arise and lead many, many, many to righteousness. This matters for all eternity. This is Christ's supreme task that He would have us all engage in. His promise is a glorious reward for all eternity. Let the wonder of Daniel 12:3 captivate your mind and spirit, that your heart would be set ablaze in passion for the gospel to be ever on your lips. Dear ones, it's time to lead many to righteousness.

> *"Arise, shine, for your light has come, and the glory of the Lord rises upon you. See, darkness covers the earth and thick darkness is over the peoples,*

but the Lord rises upon you and his glory appears over you. Nations will come to your light, and kings to the brightness of your dawn.'"
-Isaiah 60:1-3

Today is a new day of unlimited mercy and grace for you and all your heart is traversing. Is your heart all-consumed with the wonder and awe of Jesus, or do you feel tossed to and fro? I can guarantee there's a battle for your attention and affections in this hour. Where is your gaze? What's consuming your heart? May your time with the Lord minister to and reset your focus on the One deserving of a consumed life of and for Him alone.

Listen to this worship song: "Echo Holy" by Red Rocks Worship

Day Twenty-Three

---✦---

GOD SEND ME

"Then out of the smoke, one of the angels of fire flew to me. He had in his hands a burning coal he had taken from the altar with tongs. He touched my lips with it and said, 'See? The burning coal from the altar has touched your lips. Your guilt is taken away; your sin is blotted out.' Then I heard the Lord saying, 'Whom should I send to my people? Who will go to represent us?' I spoke up and said, 'I will be the one. Send me.'"
-Isaiah 6:6-8, TPT

"What if he did this to make the riches of his glory known to the objects of his mercy, whom he prepared in advance for glory … ?"
-Romans 9:23

*"How, then, can they call on the one they have not believed in?
And how can they believe in the one of whom they have not heard?
And how can they hear without someone preaching to them?
And how can anyone preach unless they are sent? As it is written:
'How beautiful are the feet of those who bring good news!'"*
-Romans 10:14-15

I have a vision brewing in my spirit. It's a movement of women all over the United States who have their affections set on Jesus and who are rallying women to get their lamps filled with oil. It's an army of revivalists who are raising up spiritual daughters who too have their eyes fixed on Jesus and their lives ablaze with His glory. The Bride, ready, walking in intimacy, is positioned in the harvest field, bringing in the great harvest. It's time.

My friend, Wade, has made a lifestyle of ministering to people in public places. Years ago, he was training himself to courageously go, he would tell his new wife, Hannah, "I am going to Walmart for two hours to pray for people and do the grocery shopping." He put it in his weekly calendar. Now, it just flows out of his life all the time. Intentionality created a lifestyle.

Last year, I met Wade at Arbor Hills Nature Park in Plano, Texas. Our plan was to pray for people and share the good news of Jesus. Upon our arrival, we immediately came across two sisters walking their dog. We asked them if we could pray for them. Karla said she wanted us to pray for their older sister, who was taking her nursing exam. After we prayed, we naturally transitioned into sharing our personal stories of when we first met Jesus. We each took just a minute to share. They listened intently. Karla had spent her life looking for God, longing for Him- not the religious works. But she didn't know how to say this to God, and no one had told her the good news of salvation. She was a nurse and worked with Christians, but none of them had shared the gospel of salvation with her.

As we explained how to know Jesus intimately, she asked, "Why wouldn't everyone want this? Will you help me to have this right now?" It was tender and sweet. We prayed with her and as the Holy Spirit filled her, she began to cry. She couldn't stop and didn't know why she was crying. She was being touched by Jesus- He was coming just like she asked. Wade and I watched Karla and her sister become miracles—from death to life.

"What if he did this to make the riches of his glory known to the objects of his mercy, whom he prepared in advance for glory ... ?"
-Romans 9:23

Each of us are objects of His mercy. We have been made glory containers. We carry His glory, His purposes, and His heart because He lives in us. Out of our life flows living waters that touch the lives of those we engage with, here and all over the world. What a joyous calling and privilege. In our American culture of individualism—and recent "social distancing"—it's intimidating to share our lives and our stories and our Jesus with people. But if the billion-soul harvest is going to be brought in, we want to be in the middle of it. I don't want to be on the bleachers cheering it on, I want to have my "beautiful feet" in the field, working and praying alongside others. Will you come with me?

The Bride is arising. I receive testimony after testimony of women whose hearts are coming alive. They are experiencing a revival of love for the One their hearts adore. The Holy Spirit is being poured out on sons and daughters, fueling courageous and passionate resolve. If this is the desire of your heart, will you say to the Lord, "I want this, Jesus. Will You do this in me? I surrender my life and plans and purposes to You today."

Do not despise the days of preparation. He will restore all the years the locusts have eaten. You have been made ready for this time in history. The harvest field needs your beautiful feet, your authority in ministry because of the places only you have walked; your hours of deep intercession for all God has called you to stand in the gap for; the tears you have sown; your voice of victorious worship; your glorious testimony that's covered in the blood of Jesus; your yes you have declared for all these years. Get ready for your yes to be answered. He has long ago put the longing in your heart to follow Him no matter where He takes you, and He will be faithful to answer it. I promise. I can testify to this truth.

So, glorious one, whose beautiful feet will bring Jesus His inheritance—the nations—it's time to get ready. Our greatest days are upon us. Throw off fear and intimidation from the spirit of darkness. There's a harvest field and a great number of women who need to be brought out of the shadows and sidelines.

"'Look at the nations and watch—and be utterly amazed.
For I am going to do something in your days that you
would not believe, even if you were told.'"
-Habakkuk 1:5

Lord, bring my sister an encounter with You this week—an encounter with Your power, Your presence, Your hope, and Your joy. Release to her a renewed calling. Strengthen her to believe You for impossibilities and to pray with a fresh gift of faith. I pray for an army of revivalists to arise all over the world—women who move and live and find their life only in You, Jesus. Pour out Your Spirit on them that they would be influencers in culture and in their nations that have been assigned to them. Give them vision and passion to see dead bones rise again. Give them vision to see what You see and to pray it forth. Lord, call forth spiritual mothers in this hour. I ask You for a movement of sold-out women—who are courageous, fearless, bold, passionate, and radical lovers of Jesus—to arise. And from this identity of Christ in them, they will be sent by Your Spirit. Call them now, in Jesus' name.

Listen to this worship song: "Gold" by Jesus Culture

Day Twenty-Four

STANDING IN A VALLEY OF PRAISE

"Early in the morning they left for the Desert of Tekoa. As they set out, Jehoshaphat stood and said, 'Listen to me, Judah and people of Jerusalem! Have faith in the Lord your God and you will be upheld; have faith in his prophets and you will be successful.' After consulting the people, Jehoshaphat appointed men to sing to the Lord and to praise him for the splendor of his holiness as they went out at the head of the army, saying: 'Give thanks to the Lord, for his love endures forever.' As they began to sing and praise, the Lord set ambushes against the men of Ammon and Moab and Mount Seir who were invading Judah, and they were defeated."
-2 Chronicles 20:20-22

I have carried this Scripture in my spirit since 2008 when I began to pray for the Church. It was such a key warfare strategy for the people of God. It is a key strategic passage for us today, as well.

Allow me to paint a picture of 2 Chronicles 20. The king was moving to turn the hearts of the people back to God in the face of an oncoming enemy. He mobilized the people, cried out to the Lord on behalf of the nation, sought the face of God in prayer, and got the army ready to move in worship. The text says,

*"All the men of Judah, with their wives and children
and little ones, stood there before the Lord."*
-2 Chronicles 20:13

A prophetic word came forth as the Spirit of God fell on one man and gave to King Jehoshaphat the play-by-play to victory.

> *"'Listen, King Jehoshaphat and all who live in Judah and Jerusalem!
> This is what the Lord says to you: "Do not be afraid or discouraged
> because of this vast army. For the battle is not yours, but God's.
> Tomorrow march down against them. They will be climbing up by
> the Pass of Ziz, and you will find them at the end of the gorge in the
> Desert of Jeruel. You will not have to fight this battle. Take up your
> positions; stand firm and see the deliverance the Lord will give you,
> Judah and Jerusalem. Do not be afraid; do not be discouraged. Go
> out to face them tomorrow, and the Lord will be with you."'"*
> -2 Chronicles 20:15-17

The threat of what they were facing was real. There was a massive army rising up against the people of God. And if God didn't rescue and save them, there was no hope. So what did the Lord tell them to do? He commanded them to get rid of fear and get ready to see deliverance. They were to prepare to see the hand of God move on behalf of their nation. How many of us in our nation are standing on the precipice of these very words! Stand firm, Church, in your position of faith, and do not be discouraged with fear. The Lord is moving on behalf of His people because He is for us and He is with us!

I can imagine some were in constant prayer and intercession. Some were probably physically preparing for war. Some were probably in a ball of tears fearing for the lives of their children. There was so much unknown. Was God really going to come through and deliver? Was the one prophet who carried the strategy to victory even trustworthy? I feel all these questions even as I write this. This is for us today—every word of this chapter.

"Early in the morning they left for the Desert of Tekoa. As they set out, Jehoshaphat stood and said, 'Listen to me, Judah and people of Jerusalem! Have faith in the Lord your God and you will be upheld; have faith in his prophets and you will be successful.'"
-2 Chronicles 20:20

The people were awakened to a new day. And this particular day was the day to head into battle and face the massive army positioned against them. God was calling for their participation. Dressed for war, he rallied them not to grab their swords or shields or an extra flask of water, but to get ready with faith. They were to have faith in what God was speaking and leading them into. This was their position and their stance and their command to believe. And what did faith release in them? The people began to worship. I have said it before and I will say it again:

The insanity of faith becomes worship that releases the fulfillment of God's promises.

"They worshipped, but why did they do it? They were not delivered. No, but they were sure they were going to be delivered. Their enemies were not dead. No, they were all alive, but they were sure they would be dead, so they had worship, and their devotion rose from trustful and grateful hearts." -Charles Spurgeon

"As they began to sing and praise, the Lord set ambushes against the men of Ammon and Moab and Mount Seir who were invading Judah, and they were defeated."
-2 Chronicles 20:22

The enemy was defeated, and the people of God didn't even raise a sword. They just had to raise a hallelujah. The people of God were merely asked to release faith and believe that God is who He said He is and will do what

He promised to do. The most amazing part of this whole battle is not only that it was just God's battle and His people's victory, but they also got the plunder of the enemy. It's like the abundant goodness of the Lord to say:

> You remain in faith, open your mouth to worship, and I will give you victory and the abundance of plunder from everything the enemy has taken.

> *"When the men of Judah came to the place that overlooks the desert and looked toward the vast army, they saw only dead bodies lying on the ground; no one had escaped. So Jehoshaphat and his men went to carry off their plunder, and they found among them a great amount of equipment and clothing and also articles of value—more than they could take away. There was so much plunder that it took three days to collect it. On the fourth day they assembled in the Valley of Berakah, where they praised the Lord. This is why it is called the Valley of Berakah to this day."*
> -2 Chronicles 20:24-26

The battle you may be facing right now or the one we are facing as a nation will be led by worshippers. The ones God is calling to the front lines are the ones who have their mouths filled with praise. It's an hour to release praise in the Earth and to agree with the plans and purposes of Heaven. He's asking for a people who will agree, not after the enemy is plundered or after we see deliverance, but before our eyes see the hand of God move.

> *"'Give thanks to the Lord, for his love endures forever.'"*
> -2 Chronicles 20:21b

As I was sitting with the Lord and penned these words He placed in my spirit:

> I am pouring out mercy—My mercy—that is not defined by worldly measures or standards. It's the mercy of another kind. It will blanket the Earth to calm the

atmosphere and push back what is being released in this hour. My mercy will put people and cities and this nation on another course toward revival. The need for me will only increase. It will not decrease. The nation and the world are longing for calm. There will be calm at times, but when I stir up hunger and desperation, it's often in the middle of the storm. Remember, the storm doesn't define the moment. My hand of righteousness, power, and mercy define the moment. I will not relent. I will not let up. But, I will continue to draw all men to Myself. This is love. I want to reveal My power and wonder to My people and to those who do not know My goodness. My faith-filled ones will be portals to release My goodness in the Earth because they are asking according to Heaven. Thy are not asking because of what they see on the Earth. They are asking according to what they know from intimacy with Me. Position yourself to receive and release. Both come out of intimacy with Me. Commune with Me.

Sister, this is our grandest moment of an invitation to faith. It's time to praise in the valley. It is time to sing our hallelujah over the plans of the enemy, over our families, over this nation, over the turmoil and traumas. A valley causes sounds to echo as they bounce off the walls or mountains around them. We can let our praise resound and be carried from this valley place. Let your worship roar in this hour as you watch God move on your behalf! Stand firm and see the deliverance of the Lord. All He asks is for you to believe Him and open your mouth to declare it. He will do the rest.

I bless you, in the name of Jesus. I bless you with a new sound in your mouth. I bless you, in Jesus' name, with faith and resolve to hold your position, standing firm in worship, no matter what your eyes see. I bless you to hear the songs that Heaven is singing over you, so you may join your voice with them. I bless you, in Jesus' name, with an extra measure of faith and for those who don't have the gift of faith, I bless you to receive the gift of faith. I bless you with strength and joy and hope and laughter in this hour because your heart is steadfast and you know in Whom you have believed. If you have entrusted Him with your eternity, you can trust Him with the list of things on your heart in this hour. I bless you with the gift of intercession and worship to conquer the plans of the enemy over your family, your calling, your city, and your nation. I bless you with increased territory of influence and the plunder from the camp of the enemy. In the glorious and abundant name of Jesus, amen.

"I felt the HOLY SPIRIT whisper to me through the weariness: 'KEEP GOING! WORSHIP IS THE KEY TO UNLOCK REVIVAL IN AMERICA!'" -Sean Feucht

Listen to this worship song: "Raise a Hallelujah" by Bethel Music

HEAR THE SOUND OF HIS MIGHTY ROAR

Do you ever wonder what the roar of God sounds like—that roar of victory for God's people? Oh, if we could just hear it with our spiritual ears. How majestic and marvelous it must be that all of Heaven and Earth pause in its glorious thunder. It's a roar not of passivity but of a conquering cry for God's people. In fact, after Jesus breathed His last on the cross, the Earth shook with a victorious thundering.

> *"Listen! Listen to the roar of his voice, to the rumbling that comes from his mouth. … After that comes the sound of his roar; he thunders with his majestic voice. When his voice resounds, he holds nothing back."*
> -Job 37:2, 4

> *"… and I saw the glory of the God of Israel coming from the east. His voice was like the roar of rushing waters, and the land was radiant with his glory."*
> -Ezekiel 43:2

> *"They will follow the Lord; he will roar like a lion. When he roars, his children will come trembling from the west."*
> -Hosea 11:10

"But the day of the Lord will come like a thief. The heavens will disappear with a roar; the elements will be destroyed by fire, and the earth and everything done in it will be laid bare."
-2 Peter 3:10

"… and he gave a loud shout like the roar of a lion. When he shouted, the voices of the seven thunders spoke."
-Revelation 10:3

In the "The Chronicles of Narnia," I love Aslan as the depiction of Jesus. It's such a beautiful picture of His power and love. Oh, but when Aslan roars, the enemy trembles. And you have to believe that Jesus is roaring for His people. For some, He is roaring for them to come awake; and for others, He's declaring His victory over your enemies.

I looked up the meaning of the word "roar" in the original language, and it is a verb which means: to roar, of a lion, conqueror, Jehovah, cry of distress, rumble or moan, mightily roar. It's not passive or descriptive in nature but rather the very action of a passionate and mighty God. He is moving and speaking and acting on your behalf. He doesn't passively sit by. He comes to your defense. Your conquering King comes with glory and power.

> He declares His roar of victory over your family!
> He declares His roar of victory over your marriage!
> He declares His roar of victory over your health!
> He declares His roar of victory over your finances!
> He declares His roar of victory over your future!

The enemy also has a voice that growls at Christ in you.

"Be alert and of sober mind. Your enemy the devil prowls around like a roaring lion looking for someone to devour."
-1 Peter 5:8

Take note that he's "like" a roaring lion, hoping we crouch in fear of him. We don't need to fear his threatening growl, but we do need to discern his words. The Bride of Christ needs the gift of wisdom and discernment right now. We need to be able to discern who is growling and speaking lies. There's a war for our faith and a war for our worship. The enemy is trying to emulate the sound of God in our ears to lead us astray. He's crafty and a liar, but he won't win. It's time to have our ears tuned sharply into the voice of God and His voice alone.

Be aware of your enemy as he's an opportunist and a savage, but his wimpy roar means nothing over your life.

Here's a portion of a recent prophetic word written by Lana Vawser. It ministered to me, and I have read it several times.

> "The Lord then showed me that these battle-weary saints have lost their ROAR in the battle. They have lost their voice and the ferociousness that they once walked in because the battle has been so intense, but the Lord is moving in power to RESTORE THE ROAR of these battle-weary ones.

> "The Lord showed me that not only is God raising them back up again in resurrection power as burning ones, burning with the fire of His love, passion, and presence, but He is raising them up in FIERCE BOLDNESS.

> "… They are the ones being sent out on assignment from the Lord with the ROAR of the Lion of Judah within them and through them that will bring an OVERTURNING to the enemy's plans. They are being sent forth as DREAD CHAMPIONS to be used by the Holy Spirit to demolish and shatter strongholds and many schemes of the enemy.

"... The Lord is restoring the roar of these battle-weary saints. No longer will they be called battle-weary, but the ferocious burning ones arising in the earth releasing the ROAR of the Lion of Judah, from the place of deep intimacy, deep humility and the sacred place of locked eyes with the One whose eyes burn with flames of fire (Revelation 19:12)." -Lana Vawser[15]

Are you ready to join your voice with His to shake foundations and declare the sounds of Heaven?

> *"After this I heard what sounded like the roar of a great*
> *multitude in heaven shouting: 'Hallelujah! Salvation*
> *and glory and power belong to our God ... .'"*
> -Revelation 19:1

> *"Then I heard what sounded like a great multitude, like the roar of rushing*
> *waters and like loud peals of thunder, shouting: 'Hallelujah! For our Lord*
> *God Almighty reigns. Let us rejoice and be glad and give him glory! For the*
> *wedding of the Lamb has come, and his bride has made herself ready.'"*
> -Revelation 19:6-7

You have a lion inside you, dear sister, who is roaring with a victory cry. It's time to join our voices with the roar of Heaven and worship Him. It's the cry of a victor giving our King His rightful adoration and praise. Nothing else in our lives deserves the worship that our victorious Warrior is due. Let's open our mouths and give Him the praise He deserves. Open your mouths and roar.

Roar in worship over your family!
Roar in worship over your city!
Roar in worship over the Bride!
Roar in worship over your nation!

Roar in worship over your destiny!

Roar in worship at our coming revival and the harvest that is already here.

Listen to this worship song: "Son of Heaven" by Brandon Lake featuring Matt Maher and Dante Bowe

Day Twenty-Six

BE STEADFAST: HE'S RUNNING TO YOU

"So is it with the resurrection of the dead. What is sown is perishable; what is raised is imperishable. It is sown in dishonor; it is raised in glory. It is sown in weakness; it is raised in power. It is sown a natural body; it is raised a spiritual body. If there is a natural body, there is also a spiritual body. …

"But thanks be to God, who gives us the victory through our Lord Jesus Christ. Therefore, my beloved brothers, be steadfast, immovable, always abounding in the work of the Lord, knowing that in the Lord your labor is not in vain."
-1 Corinthians 15:42-44, 57-58, ESV

The year 2020 was a year of shaking, and what has been most shaken, in my estimation, is the Church of Jesus Christ. God is removing, reestablishing, reckoning, and reviving His precious Bride. He is getting us ready to meet Jesus face-to-face. He is getting us ready to run into the harvest field with Him. These are days of shaking off everything that easily entangles and setting us free to go with our hearts set ablaze with the fire of the Spirit. The year 2020 was glorious on so many levels. It was the pregnant pause of preparation we desperately needed, and Jesus is running to meet us here.

For the next four chapters, we will be in 1 Corinthians 15:57-58. Today we will dive into what it looks like to be steadfast in the Lord. But first, a little context.

Paul was writing 1 Corinthians to a church that was absolutely a mess. Paul wrote the book of Corinthians from Ephesus. He had been receiving reports from people on what was taking place in the church at that time. All the issues sound familiar to the church in America today.

- They were divided along party lines.
- There were issues of sexual immorality.
- There were litigation issues among the believers.
- How about extramarital sexual unions? Yes!
- Sacrifices were made to idols.
- People ate the Lord's Supper with disregard for what it even meant.
- There were divisions among believers as many were polarized in their opinions.
- Paul encouraged them to prophesy and speak in tongues, which is a popular discussion today.

Paul gets through 14 chapters, and then, Chapter 15 becomes the most theologically meaty chapter of the whole book. Our Scripture for today has the most compelling context from which this verse is built upon. Paul reiterates the true identity of our spiritual resurrection. As we have been buried with Christ, we have been raised with Christ. Everything he writes in verses 42-44 is true of us today spiritually and will be true of us when Jesus comes for His Bride. Paul set the vision before the church, essentially saying, "Here is your true identity and the vision before you: Jesus is coming back."

In order to get to the verses at the end of the Chapter 15, we have to understand what was in Paul's heart. Suddenly, all the crazy he was addressing came into view; it funneled down. It was as though the clouds parted, and his words of vision fell on this letter to the church in Corinth. Listen, you stand firm in the gospel—it was your salvation (1 Corinthians 15:1-2), but you also stand in victory. Death has been defeated. Not only that, Jesus is coming back for His Bride, and we've got to get this reality in view. I almost hear the words of John 9:4—work while it is still day with eyes on the coming resurrection.

And then come these words:

> *"Therefore, my beloved brother, be steadfast ... ."*
> -1 Corinthians 15:58

To be steadfast denotes to sit, to be settled and established. We are seated with Christ. It comes out of a place of rest—not striving and straining, pacing and fretting. It's from our seated position in Christ and being firmly established in Him.

This is your firmest position: seated in Christ, established in Him, dwelling in the shelter of the Most High God. Nothing can snatch you from Him. No one can render your identity and inheritance in the Lord null and void. You are bought and sealed. It's a done deal. But the sanctification of becoming like Him is where we find ourselves in this moment. He responds to hunger. He responds to even a mustard seed of faith from one who says, "Jesus, take me deeper."

You are *"steadfast"* according to your spiritual position in Christ. You are *"in the Lord."* He is coming back for you. So therefore, what is truest today for those whose gazes are fixed, who are longing for Him and expectant of His coming? What is true for the army of women God is raising up in this hour to carry revival?

> "Our Father delights in, takes pleasure in and is favorably
> inclined towards us: we are His children. You who fear
> the Lord and honor His name, be so encouraged. The

Scripture declares that books of remembrance are being written for you who fear and honor the Lord's name. You are a prized possession of the Lord. You are a treasure worth more than all treasures of the earth combined. The Lord delights in you. The Father is favorably inclined toward you. Lift your head, raise up the banner, for His banner over you is love." -Christina McCracken[16]

From this theological position, you get to thrive. The abundance of Heaven is at your disposal. We are learning how to pray into and access all Christ has given to us. This does not mean we are not pruned for increase. This does not mean we don't experience pain as we move from glory to glory. We are being aligned with what is true of us so that we live out of this reality. That is why it is vital to do this spiritual journey of dependency and worship and intimacy with one another. We spur each other on in our life with Christ.

My dear friend, Susan, was battling for her life as cancer invaded her whole body. This is part of her testimony:

"The only constant in my life was the Lord, and He showed Himself to me as El Shaddai—God Almighty. He met me in the dark nights when pain prevented sleep, and He comforted me with a knowing in my spirit that He was there and wouldn't leave me. His beautiful and kind presence was what I clung to when there was no one else who could grasp the agony of my affliction and bring peace. I found His sufficiency to be more than what I needed. I know I have grown in my relationship with Jesus over the past two years, and there is more to discover. He only limits Himself in that which He is willing to share based on how much of Him I am willing to know."

Take a minute, take a deep breath, and create a space of stillness. Visually see yourself tucked into Christ, standing with Him on the water's edge of an endless ocean. You and Jesus standing there together. His arms are around you, and His eyes are filled with love. He looks at you as He beckons you to the invitation of a lifetime:

> Will you dare to dive into the expanse of Who I am and all I have for you?

You are looking with Him at the enormous ocean lapping your toes. It's an endless ocean where you get to scour the depth of the goodness, power, love, and truth of our Father, Jesus, and Holy Spirit. Do you want it? It's yours for the taking. It's an invitation to adventure and intimacy like nothing else. Will you dive into this ocean and go where you've never gone before? I promise, it's worth it. He will be with you, there's nothing to fear.

This is the vision I experienced with the Lord in 2008. The scene was what I saw and the words I heard in my spirit. And it was an invitation that required faith to say, "yes." I knew He was trustworthy. He is still pursuing my heart and your heart. He wants all of you, and I bet you want all He wants to give you. Let's become the strong Church that God intended for His Son Jesus. Let's give Him permission today to do what only He can do in and through our lives for the sake of His kingdom and purposes.

> I bless you in the name of Jesus with a depth of desire for Him like you have not yet experienced. So much awaits you. He's running.

Listen to this worship song: "To You" by Maverick City Music

IMMOVABILITY: ROOTS AND CROWNS

"But thanks be to God, who gives us the victory through our Lord Jesus Christ. Therefore, my beloved brothers, be steadfast, immovable, always abounding in the work of the Lord, knowing that in the Lord your labor is not in vain."
-1 Corinthians 15:57-58, ESV

In 1 Corinthians 15, Paul sets our eyes on our spiritual identity of being resurrected with Christ. He also wants our eyes fixed forward in faith at our coming resurrection when Christ comes for His Bride. We stand in the "now and not yet" of this spiritual reality. Therefore, how do we live "in the Lord"? Immovable.

Immovable means not being moved from your place. It's a firmly persistent position. It's the conviction Paul wrote to Timothy: *"That is why I am suffering as I am. Yet this is no cause for shame, because I know whom I have believed, and am convinced that he is able to guard what I have entrusted to him until that day (2 Timothy 1:12)."* Our resolute conviction and confidence are in the One our hearts adore—in the One who gave us His victory.

- In prison, Joseph was immovable because God gave him a dream to hold on to.

- In prison, Paul and Silas could worship until the prison doors flew open because their eyes were fully fixed on Jesus.
- In the fiery furnace, Shadrach, Meshach and Abednego could say, *"If we are thrown into the blazing furnace, the God we serve is able to deliver us from it, and he will deliver us from Your Majesty's hand. But even if he does not, we want you to know, Your Majesty, that we will not serve your gods or worship the image of gold you have set up (Daniel 3:17-18)."*

"Steadfast" and "immovable" are two common words that accompany my prayers for the Bride of Christ. The Lord has expanded my language to include "oaks of righteousness" as it pertains to these two words. Do you know what the root system of an oak tree looks like? According to Garden Guides, "Oak trees develop very deep rooting systems that branch off its main taproot. Over time, the taproot's prominence recedes and is replaced by numerous large lateral roots that form the lateral root system. These lateral roots penetrate the soil 4 feet deep and extend laterally to 90 feet."[17] The lateral roots can expand four to seven times the width of the tree's crown. The roots anchor the oak into immovability.

> *"They will be called oaks of righteousness, a planting*
> *of the Lord for the display of his splendor."*
> -Isaiah 61:3b

My spirit is alive with these words:

> Oaks of righteousness are established in our nation (and the nations) and are about ready to release fruit in the Earth. They aren't there to just look pretty. There's a reason I call them "oaks of righteousness"—they are significant to the landscape (spiritual landscape) of a nation. And they are immovable even in a storm.

Sister, God has called you an oak of righteousness. He has made you immovable in Him—no one can snatch you from His hand. It's what is true of you if your life is anchored in Christ and His Word lives in you. When my daughter, AnnMarie, was in middle school, she asked me to do a discipleship group with her friends. She wanted them to have deep roots in Jesus. We would meet every week, and I remember one common theme the Lord continually prompted in my heart for them:

Get the Word of God inside you!

There may come a time when it is no longer legal for us to have the Word of God. You see this in many nations around the world. We must get it in us now. We must hide it in us so that we live from this place of truth.

Many, many believers will fall away from the truth of God's Word. They will become captivated with hollow philosophy (Colossians 2:8), antichrist theologies (1 John 4:3), and worldly beliefs (Titus 2:11-14). Just one degree off and then another and then another, and we have become captivated with what could sound like Jesus but is not. Beloved, we need to be immovable in the Word of God in this hour. We need the gift of discernment and wisdom like never before. Your roots in the Word must expand across the landscape of your life and grow to a deeper depth than yesterday. I say this with an urgency even as I pray this for my own daughters, my husband, myself, and for you.

> *"Let me describe the one who truly follows me and does what I say.*
> *He is like a man who chooses the right place to build a house and then*
> *lays a deep and secure foundation. When the storms and floods rage*
> *against that house, it continues to stand strong and unshaken through*
> *the tempest, for he built it wisely on the right foundation. But the*
> *one who has heard my teaching and does not obey it is like a man*
> *who builds a house without laying any foundation at all. When the*

storms and floods rage against that house, it will immediately collapse
and become a total loss. Which of these two builders will you be?'"
-Luke 6:47-49, TPT

Get your tools in hand—it's time to dig, and it's time to build. He has a crown to display in your life.

> "This invitation upon us right now in this new era is to decide to take our stand upon the Word of God like never before. This era of unprecedented displays of His power and miracles is going to come through a people who live, breathe, feast, and walk upon the Word of God and live from that place. ... So by the power of the Word of God and by faith we root and anchor our expectancy." -Lana Vawser[18]

Jesus counsels us in truth by the Spirit who lives in us. He leads us and shows us what is true and what is false. He uses the hard things we have walked through to expand and deepen our faith and belief in the Word of God and the truth of His character. He prunes us, and the places that have been tried and tested become our greatest deposit of faith and authority. We go deep not so we go underground and become less present in the world. We go deep so the crown of our tree gets wider for an even greater display of His glory. Our leaves are for the healing of nations (Revelation 22:2). We are planted by streams of living water, bearing fruit in and out of season (Psalm 1:3). We are rooted and built up in Him, strengthened in the faith as you were taught, and overflowing with thankfulness (Colossians 2:7).

For those God is leading to lie beside quiet waters for restoration, take this time and just receive from the Lord. Rest and peace are yours. Let your roots go deep into His presence where your soul is restored. Your taproot system, just like the oak tree, is looking for living water so that your lateral root system can anchor your growth. Receive what God is doing in you; you are going to need it for future ministry and fruitfulness. The leaves of healing that will burst forth in your life for people and nations matter now as your roots are growing down deep. The faith that will come forth from this season of rest and restoration will be exponentially greater than you could have imagined. I prophesy that your faith will be expansive. You will believe for impossibility and even greater things at a much more rapid rate. You will not second guess what God speaks or what He calls you to do or to pray. Faith will become second nature.

I want to pray for those who are incredibly hungry for the Lord. He is preparing a table before you, and it will be a feast of His goodness and healing. You have not walked this road before, but the Lord is leading you to walk to His banqueting table, and His banner over you is love. He is attracted to hunger and is answering the ultimate desires of your heart.

> I pray for perseverance and increased desire for You, Jesus. I pray for the spirit of wisdom and discernment to fall upon you in greater measure. I ask, Lord, for counsel by Your Spirit to know what is true and what is false. I pray for a sensitivity to Your Spirit that is a gift. I pray for deep roots and a crowned tree that bears fruit in every season. Lord, for the one who needs healing physically, spiritually, and emotionally, I pray You would release this as she brings YYou her faith and her hearts' greatest desires. And as she waits for You to move, teach her how to live in grace and how to receive Your mercy every day. Confound her with Your goodness, Jesus! Make her head spin at Your wonders. May she have eyes to see and lips to declare the magnificence and power of who You are and what You are doing. Make her an overcomer by the blood of the Lamb and the word of her testimony. May Your goodness and Your glory rest on her today so that searching people can

build a nest in the branches of her crown and encounter You. In the precious name of Jesus, amen!

Listen to this worship song: "Surrounded (Fight My Battles)" by Bethel Music featuring Kari Jobe

Day Twenty-Eight

---❀---

ABOUNDING IN THIS HOUR

*"But thanks be to God, who gives us the victory through our
Lord Jesus Christ. Therefore, my beloved brothers, be steadfast,
immovable, always abounding in the work of the Lord,
knowing that in the Lord your labor is not in vain."*
-1 Corinthians 15:57-58, ESV

Paul calls believers to their now and not yet reality of their resurrection. And therefore, from this position, we are steadfast (seated, settled, and established), immovable (not being moved from your place, firmly persistent), and abounding.

The word "abounding" means outstanding, abundant, overflowing, to superabound in quantity or quality, be in excess, having more abundance, exceed, excel, increase. This only comes from being in the Lord. It's in Him, of Him, and through Him. None of it is done outside of surrender and dependence on the life of Christ in you and through you. We can work and produce out of our excellence and giftedness, but the excess and the abundance and the increase only come from Him. And it's eternal when it comes from Him. It is Christ in me and Christ through me that brings the abounding.

Look at this beautiful picture of abounding in the midst of uncertainty from Acts 28. Paul shipwrecked on the Island of Malta. He swam to shore and was cold and most likely exhausted from the ordeal. As Paul helped to build the fire, he was bitten by a viper. The snake was literally hanging from his hand. Can you not imagine the annoyance of one circumstance after another for Paul? Paul didn't get sick or die from the snakebite, which won the favor the islanders. The poison did not harm him, miraculously. He was welcomed to the estate of the chief official of the island, whose father was sick. God showed up in all His goodness and healed the sick man. Paul stepped into a moment where I could guess his flesh was weak, but Christ in him abounded. And not only did God heal one man through Paul, all the sick on the island were brought to him and were healed. Paul experienced abounding fruitfulness in the midst of disheartening circumstances.

All the circumstances Paul experienced continued to open his eyes to the wonder and presence of God. What the enemy kept throwing at him, God continued to turn for His glory. What if we looked at every circumstance that was thrown at us in 2020 and looked for His glory—the very story He is setting up for the end-time harvest and the return of Jesus.

> "There's a whole lot of shakin' going on, and God Himself is behind much of it. World orders will rise and fall as convulsions of history collapse upon one another, because the kingdom of heaven is putting unbearable pressure on the structure of hell as Jesus draws near. This is the best hour to be alive, and you need to know that remnants make a difference. Great doors swing on little hinges. The history of acts of God are tied into the little things that make a big difference." -Lance Wallnau[19]

Two years ago, Arise was birthed from the heart of God to call women out of the shadows and onto the front lines. Jesus was the first liberator of women, and it is His desire that we walk in all He paid for on the cross for our freedom and our identity as a daughter with the DNA of Jesus pulsating through our blood. We are not second class with a lesser calling or smaller portion of the Holy Spirit. Women have been oppressed all over the world in the name of Christendom, and it breaks the heart of God. It's His desire that we flourish, thrive, increase, abound, excel, and exceed the limitations the world, the enemy, or even lies we have believed. It's our hour to arise and take hold of all God has for His name's sake and for our abundance. I think we all want to take hold of that truth and let it catapult us into a new level of worship, faith, and response. But how do we get there? How do we get from our metaphorical point A to point B?

Surrender.

God has to do exceedingly more. He has to move us from glory to glory. We merely cooperate and respond. We move into a posture of surrender and let God speak and turn and shift and bring forth impossibilities. Every day, in every stage, trial, and season, we have an opportunity to press into Jesus or take the road of least resistance. It's the cry of my heart to ask the Lord to take me where He desires. Ultimately, I know it will be the most fulfilling. He has the best plans and ideas. Let's ask Him for new levels of healing and faith to embrace the new place He is taking us. Let's worship Him longer and choose to not give up in the face of discouragement. It's not a choice for those of us whose hearts are set on Jesus to choose the ways of the world or our little kingdoms. That type of surrender is not an option. The surrender that comes out of sowing seed, worshipping in spite of feeling dry or conflicted, praising God in pain, or choosing Jesus over soothing our flesh, is where radical responses to the Holy Spirit are born. And out of that response, comes abounding. Paul could have sat in self-pity on that island, out of disillusionment and sheer exhaustion, but he chose to step in believing that God had something there for him, too. Nothing is happenstance. Nothing is coincidence in the life of the believer. And in those shipwrecked moments of life, we either sink to the bottom or swim in the vast goodness of God.

Surrender is when we live with the mentality that God is in every detail of our lives and, therefore, can be trusted. Our invitation is to find Him on this treasure island.

Beloved, where we are going will require unfaltering partnership with Father, Jesus, and Holy Spirit. It will require Him shaking off everything that entangles us, and us letting go. It will require the freedom Jesus purchased for you with His very life. It will require faith for impossibility, that He gives to you as a gift. Do you see these are things God does, but we receive them? None of these things are possible in our humanity, they are only possible because of the cross. Our resurrection with Christ intersects our surrender; Jesus is allowed to take over, and you come behind Him, anchor yourself in Him, and follow the One your heart truly desires. The life of abounding and abundance follows surrender and dependency. That's the beautiful dance of partnership with the Lord. There is no striving, straining, or legalistic obedience. It's about the responsiveness of the life of a daughter to the abundance of her Father.

"You have my yes before you even ask." This is what I am praying is the declaration written over our lives. I pray that He moves us from one yes to the next yes, all our days. I wish I could sit across from you and ask, "Will you invite the Lord to title His scroll of remembrance over your life with these words: 'She gave me her yes before I even asked'?" From our position of surrender to Christ, being rooted and built up in Him, we abound with fruitfulness and life we couldn't ever have done on our own. Surrender and abounding dance together so beautifully. And it's in this truth, that the glory of God is made manifest in your life and mine.

Would you pray, "Lord, You have my yes before You even ask"? And with open hands of surrender, ask the Lord to do in and through you what you could never do even on your best day. Ask Him to begin to release the plans He has written over your life before the foundations of the world were laid. He's inviting you to arise in this hour to carry forth exploits that are in His heart that will shift generations and nations.

> "Women, arise and shine for the glory of God is upon you. It is your season, it is your turn, it is your time. Walk together with faithful men and carry this glorious Gospel. I know that Jesus is calling all of us to have more oil and to be His light on earth and His salt in the earth. We call half of the population, which is female, to rise up and carry the glory of God!" -Patricia King[20]

Listen to this worship song: "Heart and Hands" by Sean Feucht

Day Twenty-Nine

---✤---

YOUR LABOR AND YOUR TRIUMPH

"But thanks be to God, who gives us the victory through our
Lord Jesus Christ. Therefore, my beloved brothers, be steadfast,
immovable, always abounding in the work of the Lord,
knowing that in the Lord your labor is not in vain."
-1 Corinthians 15:57-58, ESV

The word "labor" is associated with grief, sorrow, and even trouble. The meaning behind this statement is that your labor in the Lord is not empty or resulting in nothing. Interesting that Paul doesn't disregard this intimate part of being seated, persistent, and firm, increasing and overflowing, and yet Jesus said, *"'In this world you will have trouble. But take heart! I have overcome the world (John 16:33).'"* Yes, victory is ours, immovability is ours, increase is ours. And yet in this world our labor or work can have pain, tears, and suffering associated with it.

My best friend from college, Kel, and her husband, Scott, had a daughter 13 years ago. It was a difficult pregnancy, so she and Scott decided to adopt three more children. They received three more children—two boys and a girl—each two years apart. Their family looks like Heaven with all the different skin colors. By the time one of their sons was 6, he began manifesting very disruptive and potentially violent behavior. It wreaked havoc on their family, and Scott and Kel had to admit him to an extended behavioral and mental health treatment program.

They had been in limited contact with the birth mom over the years but had asked several times unsuccessfully about medical history to gain a better understanding of their son's issues. Finally, in a last plea while taking their son to the hospital again, the birth mom admitted to taking drugs while she was pregnant. His little brain was damaged, and his emotional growth altered. Kel and Scott were devastated and heartbroken for their son. In their grief and in deep despair, Scott sensed the Lord placing these words on his heart:

> If she would have told you at the beginning, you would have not taken him.

It was God's goodness to their son that, in His mercy, He chose Scott and Kel to parent him.

They said, "Yes," to this calling when the Lord put it before them. Now the grace for walking out their calling will need to come in even greater measure. Being in the Lord and trusting what you've heard clearly does not mean it won't come without tears and pain. In fact, you can count on two things: every calling will be tested, and there will be a battle before every breakthrough. He sees the finished prize, and yet He rejoices in the process. He is faithful to carry us to the finish line. No one and nothing can snatch you from the hand of God. Come hell or high water, you are in Him, sealed with His Spirit, and He's coming back for you.

Your labor and your pain in the Lord is not in vain, dear sister.

I need you to hear these words because as we move from glory to glory, we become more like Jesus. He takes the areas of our lives that need to be shaped and pruned and purified, and if we will hand them to Him, He will put His glory on them. And we will look more and more like Jesus. Your pain and grief and sorrow are not in vain because you are in the Lord. Your God will never fail you; He will never forsake His own.

Your triumph was written by the blood of Jesus on the cross.

"And what more shall I say? I do not have time to tell about Gideon, Barak, Samson and Jephthah, about David and Samuel and the prophets, who through faith conquered kingdoms, administered justice, and gained what was promised; who shut the mouths of lions, quenched the fury of the flames, and escaped the edge of the sword; whose weakness was turned to strength; and who became powerful in battle and routed foreign armies. Women received back their dead, raised to life again. There were others who were tortured, refusing to be released so that they might gain an even better resurrection. Some faced jeers and flogging, and even chains and imprisonment. They were put to death by stoning; they were sawed in two; they were killed by the sword. They went about in sheepskins and goatskins, destitute, persecuted and mistreated—the world was not worthy of them. They wandered in deserts and mountains, living in caves and in holes in the ground. These were all commended for their faith, yet none of them received what had been promised, since God had planned something better for us so that only together with us would they be made perfect."
-Hebrews 11:32-40

If you trust Him for the victory, will you trust Him in the trial?

"So David triumphed over the Philistine with a sling and a stone; without a sword in his hand he struck down the Philistine and killed him."
-1 Samuel 17:50

Do you know that David was anointed as King when he was just a teenager tending sheep during the day? It was soon after that he faced Goliath, was run off by Saul, found his place of hiding in the desert, lived on the run from his enemies, was forced out of Israel, and fought many battles along the way. It took 15 years of preparation between the time he was anointed king and became king of the nation Israel. We so want the crown and not the years of preparation. We question and complain and weep and toil, waiting for the promise to be fulfilled. And Jesus looks at us and says He is our promise, and everything is fulfilled in Him. His triumph is written over your life, your salvation, your journey to healing, your wholeness, and your final crowning before the Bema Seat of Christ. This journey of surrender and sanctification as we are in the Lord matters to God. It really matters to God.

Even when we are walking in perfect union with Father, Jesus, and Holy Spirit, we are going to face toil and trial. We will begin to view it from the perspective of God the more we walk with Him in deeper intimacy. We will realize the necessity of gratitude to be the gamechanger for acceptance and embrace. And on the flip side of the pain will be the redemption of God. He will cause the pain and suffering to bring the overflow and even greater authority for ministry. The Lord is enlarging our capacity to carry more of His manifest power and presence through our lives. The year 2020 was a divine reset for the Bride of Christ. None of what you have gone through or are going through is in vain because you are in the Lord. But if it is not processed by the Word of God and the counsel of the Holy Spirit, this is where ungodly beliefs can begin to shape our faith.

So today, let's stand on the precipice of our tumultuous days and give Him praise. He knows how this story ends. And just like Scott and Kel who are believing for the healing of their son, until we see that day come, our only option is to praise Him.

> *"Consider it pure joy, my brothers and sisters, whenever you face trials of many kinds, because you know that the testing of your faith produces perseverance. Let perseverance finish its work so that you may be mature and complete, not lacking anything."*
> -James 1:2-4

He is making you complete so you will not lack anything. And the outcome of the pain is that He will redeem and return to you sevenfold what the enemy has stolen. Take heart; you are secure in Him and He is for you. Today, let's just praise Him and give Him thanks for His triumph and tenderness to His beloved Bride.

I want to close with a Scripture that has shown up in my life several times as I took hold of this promise. A harvest of joy and reaping is coming forth from you. So hold tight, sister, and do not let go of the Lord in this hour.

"When the Lord restored the fortunes of Zion, we were like those who dreamed. Our mouths were filled with laughter, our tongues with songs of joy. Then it was said among the nations, 'The Lord has done great things for them.' The Lord has done great things for us, and we are filled with joy.

"Restore our fortunes, Lord, like streams in the Negev. Those who sow with tears will reap with songs of joy. Those who go out weeping, carrying seed to sow, will return with songs of joy, carrying sheaves with them."
-Psalm 126

Listen to this worship song: "See a Victory" by Elevation Worship

---

A Glorious Gift is Coming

"In the morning, Lord, you hear my voice; in the morning
I lay my requests before you and wait expectantly."
-Psalm 5:3

According to Strong's Concordance, the word "expectantly" means to look out or about, spy, keep watch, observe, watch, or watch closely. It denotes leaning forward, to peer into the distance. We are waiting in expectation for the righteous hand of God to move with power. Everything He does is wrapped in His love, and He's moving on behalf of His Bride. Look up, dear sister. He's on His way, just like He was for the wise men who were waiting in expectation for their King.

The word in my spirit going into 2020 was "wonder," along with this passage from Isaiah:

"And the Lord said: 'Because this people draw near with their mouth
and honor me with their lips, while their hearts are far from me,
and their fear of me is a commandment taught by men, therefore,
behold, I will again do wonderful things with this people, with
wonder upon wonder; and the wisdom of their wise men shall perish,
and the discernment of their discerning men shall be hidden.'"
-Isaiah 29:13-14, ESV

I believe God is releasing a new wave across the Earth, especially as it pertains to His Bride. This wave is a holy fear of the Lord. It's not about Him being angry with us, but rather about consecration and holiness and purity for the people of God. These are the words He placed on my heart:

> A fear of the Lord is being established in the hearts of My people. It is what I am doing, not as a result of the forces of darkness. My people need this because they are floundering. They have been taught to trust and believe a very small God. How do you trust a God who has been minimized to humanity? I will change their perceptions. They need to know who I really Am and that they can trust Me. I am good, and My love endures forever. But I also mean what I say. Christianity isn't some kind of game or social group; it is a life of intimacy with Me, the God of the universe. The church has made Me so small. I am He, and there is no other. I will not be mocked. I will not be silent or silenced in the Earth. My roar will be heard, and My people will respond in worship. Do not fear the terror of day. Fear the Lord and His power! Receive the gift of the fear of the Lord as it covers the Earth like a blanket. Fear the Lord, all you people. The fear of the Lord will cover the Earth like a canopy. It is coming. Prepare your heart to receive it. Open your hands, and I will deposit it deep inside of you like a gift from Me. It will transform My people and set them free from their prison of small thinking.

God, touch our lives with a reverence and an awe and a fear of the Lord in this hour.

"And Mary sang this song: 'My soul is ecstatic, overflowing with praises to God! My spirit bursts with joy over my life-giving God! For he set his

tender gaze upon me, his lowly servant girl. And from here on, everyone will know that I have been favored and blessed. The Mighty One has worked a mighty miracle for me; holy is his name! Mercy kisses all who fear him, from one generation to the next. Mighty power flows from him to scatter all those who walk in pride. Powerful princes he tears from their thrones and he lifts up the lowly to take their place. Those who hunger for him will always be filled, but the smug and self-satisfied he will send away empty. Because he can never forget to show mercy, he has helped his chosen servant, Israel, keeping his promises to Abraham and to his descendants forever."
-Luke 1:46-55, TPT

As a simple servant girl was called by her Father, encountered by the Holy Spirit, and called to carry Jesus within her womb, her offering to Him was humility and her yes. He came and overshadowed her. Can you even imagine the fear of the Lord that she walked in, gifted by Him, as Heaven touched Earth? She didn't have to muster it in her flesh because she knew exactly Who she had believed and that nothing was impossible with God.

We come to this season of expectation when this whole year has been shaken. God will confound the wisdom of the Earth and He will confound those who confess Him with only empty words. He will forever be a God of wonder. He will forever be the God who moves ahead of us to make level ground and open prison doors. He does not want us stuck in small thinking or held in captivity. He died so we could encounter Him in every moment and in every detail of our lives. No more being held imprisoned in small thinking, in Jesus' name.

When I was summitting Kilimanjaro a few years ago, we started at midnight in order to summit at 8 a.m. At about 3 a.m., I began throwing up. One of our guides named Emmanuel began to walk with me. He took my pack from me. I would throw up and he would wipe my mouth and give me water. It was humbling, and yet I needed his help to get to the top. As we walked, he began to sing "Amazing Grace" in Swahili. My Emmanuel was making His presence and love known through his African son, who was giving him the grace to care for me all the way to the top.

Beloved, this is our nation. God did not forget us in the mountainous climb of 2020 and beyond. Have you caught His tender gaze? His grace is sufficiently carrying us, but He has more for us. He has a summit ahead for you that will mark you forever. But it begins and ends with Him.

Do you remember where you were when He first called you to Himself? He was intimate and wooing. And He still is. But He also wants to take you deeper and deeper into holiness and purity, where your life is consumed with only Him. Mary didn't mind the ridicule from Nazareth because she had an encounter that made her ready for the sacrifice. The fear of the Lord that God is wanting to deposit in His people will be a gift to us. The places in our heart that need a reset or an uprooting will be overwhelmed with who He is. It's good and right. What needs to stay will grow and flourish and thrive. What needs to go will go by His grace.

Let this encounter from Song of Solomon give you an explicit picture of His pursuing love for you. He will come with passion, and He comes with invitation to you today.

The Shulamite Bride

"After this I let my devotion slumber, but my heart for him stayed awake. I had a dream. I dreamed of my beloved—he was coming to me in the darkness of night. The melody of the man I love awakened me. I heard his knock at my heart's door as he pleaded with me:

The Bridegroom-King

"Arise, my love. Open your heart, my darling, deeper still to me. Will you receive me this dark night? There is no one else but you, my friend, my equal. I need you this night to arise and come be with me.

You are my pure, loyal dove, a perfect partner for me. My flawless one, will you arise? For my heaviness and tears are more than I can bear. I have spent myself for you throughout the dark night."
-Song of Songs 5:2, TPT

Sister, it's time to hold nothing back as we summit this season of revival. Let Him carry you and speak tenderly to you today. Withhold nothing as He searches your heart. This gift of a fear of the Lord is holy and is coming to those with longing to receive it. It's our new beginning. It's our wisdom for the coming days. It's our place of refuge and belonging.

> Father, I pray for Your daughter today. Make her ready to receive a greater depth of knowledge and calling to fear the Lord as a daughter and saint. I pray for humility and surrender to open wide her hands and her mouth that You would fill her with a glorious declaration of Who You are! Anoint her with eyes to see Your tender gaze and wondrous love for her. Completely undo her, Jesus, so that this becomes a time of worship and awe and wonder, in the glorious name of Jesus!

Listen to this worship song: "When I Lock Eyes with You" by Maverick City Music and Upperroom

Day Thirty-One

SPIRITUAL WOMBS

*"During the sixth month of Elizabeth's pregnancy, the angel
Gabriel was sent from God's presence to an unmarried girl named
Mary, living in Nazareth, a village in Galilee. She was engaged to
a man named Joseph, a true descendant of King David. Gabriel
appeared to her and said, 'Rejoice, beloved young woman, for the
Lord is with you and so you are anointed with great favor.'*

*"Mary was deeply troubled over the words of the angel and bewildered
over what this may mean for her. But the angel reassured her, saying,
'Do not yield to your fear, Mary, for the Lord has found delight in you
and has chosen to surprise you with a wonderful gift. You will become
pregnant with a baby boy, and you are to name him Jesus. He will be
supreme and will be known as the Son of the Highest. And the Lord
God will enthrone him as King on the throne of his ancestor David. He
will reign as King of Israel forever, and his reign will have no limit.'*

"Mary said, 'But how could this happen? I am still a virgin!'

*"Gabriel answered, 'The Spirit of Holiness will fall upon you and almighty
God will spread his shadow of power over you in a cloud of glory! This is
why the child born to you will be holy, and he will be called the Son of
God. What's more, your aged aunt, Elizabeth, has also become pregnant*

with a son. The "barren one" is now in her sixth month. Not one promise
from God is empty of power, for nothing is impossible with God!'

"Then Mary responded, saying, 'Yes! I will be a mother for the Lord!
As his servant, I accept whatever he has for me. May everything
you have told me come to pass.' And the angel left her."
-Luke 1:26-38, TPT

Oh, the anticipation of marriage Mary must have felt. The day was coming when she and her beloved Joseph would consummate what God had brought together. Perhaps she was counting down the days in both anticipation and timidity. And one day the angel appeared to her and intercepted her whole life. Her betrothal, marriage, and wedding night were not going to be the normal plan of events any longer. In fact, she would supernaturally carry within her the very life of Heaven. The Holy Spirit would come, anoint her with favor, overshadow her, and touch her womb with life. Everything would look so different for Mary, but she didn't hesitate. Faith surrounded her for the glorious impossibility of God.

Mary offered her womb to God for the very person of Christ to be born through.

She was called and commissioned by the God of the universe for an impossible task only He could do. And she was called to it before the foundations of the Earth were laid. She was called, but God had to fulfill the calling. I believe the Lord prepared her heart for the invitation and knew the humility He gifted her with would be the fertile soil for the promise to be planted within. Her spiritual womb had been prepared in advance of the physical manifestation of this life inside her. And a response of worship was all she wanted to give. I can only imagine what Her yes sounded like as it reverberated throughout Heaven. I wonder if the angels matched it with a symphony unheard of through all the ages. We know a song was being written in her (Luke 1:46-55).

Mary's life was an offering to Heaven.

She had two things to give the Lord in His glorious invitation to bear His Son. She had her yes, and she had her womb. Her agreement and her body were presented to the Lord in an offering that changed everything for humanity.

This is so profound to me. God comes to us with an invitation and asks us if we will give our yes and our lives to contain the yes. Will we give God our yes no matter the sacrifice or the shame or scorn? Will we give God our yes when He asks for the physical sacrifice demanded of us? Can God have our worship when it costs us everything? Can He have our faith when He calls us to do something in which we have zero experience or context for understanding? What if we looked at the invitation and we pictured the womb of Mary and with immediacy declared, "Nothing is impossible with God"?

We partner with God to birth the things of God through our spiritual wombs.

God prepares our spiritual wombs for both assignments and callings.

He gets us ready to receive the seed of invitation in agreement with our yes. From there, the Holy Spirit overshadows us with the grace to walk out what God desires to bring forth. He sanctifies us as we carry Jesus into the calling. He nourishes our very life with His Word and His presence, creating an environment for the calling to grow into fulfillment. And life comes forth that has the DNA of Heaven on it. And we wonder at the goodness and the faithfulness of God to bring forth something of such great worth from our simple offering of our lives.

I have many dear friends who have given God their yes, no matter the cost. And they wait and they wait for the fulfillment of that baby coming forth from their lives. In the meantime, He gives them dreams of being pregnant to keep their hearts and minds focused on the fact that He is at work creating within them the life of Christ that will impact generations and cities and marketplaces and nations.

God is touching spiritual wombs and making us pregnant with His purposes in this hour!

My friend Celeste shared, "The Lord is leading me to say, 'Yes,' but I don't know what that looks like." Amen! We don't have to know what Jesus will look like when the promise comes forth. He just needs to hear that we trust Him and our lives are offerings we lay at His feet. Today, consider saying to the Lord, "Make me pregnant with your purposes, God." I am sure Mary was intimidated by the encounter she was given, but her faith arose, and she gave God her life and her womb for His purposes.

> *"'From the east I summon a bird of prey; from a far-off land,*
> *a man to fulfill my purpose. What I have said, that I will*
> *bring about; what I have planned, that I will do.'"*
> -Isaiah 46:11

> *"The Lord said to me, 'You have seen correctly, for I*
> *am watching to see that my word is fulfilled.'"*
> -Jeremiah 1:12

> *"You keep every promise you've ever made to me! Since*
> *your love for me is constant and endless, I ask you, Lord,*
> *to finish every good thing that you've begun in me!"*
> -Psalm 138:8, TPT

> *"The Lord will accomplish what concerns me; Your faithfulness,*
> *Lord, is everlasting; Do not abandon the works of Your hands."*
> -Psalm 138:8, NASB

"There's been an intense battle over a 'word of the Lord' in the lives of many which has escalated intensely over the last few months. This battle has been fierce not only because of the incredible demonstration of His power and faithfulness to you in Him fulfilling that which He has spoken, but the MANIFESTATION of what HE has spoken in your life is going to change the trajectory of your life in such a significant way, which will move you into the glorious unexpected directions of the Lord's hand." - Lana Vawser[21]

The cross was a womb for new life.

In Mary's womb and on the cross on Golgotha, life was born for all humanity. The womb of a woman and the womb of a cross bore us life. In our spiritual birth and in the losing of our lives for His life, we find true life. We have an invitation as followers of Jesus to go with Him no matter what it costs because in losing our lives, we find Him. In laying down our agendas, we pick up the agenda of Heaven. In laying down our fear or hesitancy at the feet of Jesus as worship, He places His blood and His freedom and His power on us and calls us into His greater purposes. It's what He does. And today, we get to offer Him the wombs of our lives for His life to be born inside us and through us. Wonder overshadows us when in humility we let Him do whatever He wants to do. In cancer. In calling. In job transition. In barrenness. In suffering. All these places are spiritual wombs for the life of Christ to be implanted. So let's pray together for these things and ask Him to anoint them.

> Jesus, I bring to You this morning my spiritual womb that perhaps feels barren or one that is full that I don't want to carry any longer. I pray, Jesus, for a touch of Your favor and anointing over my life—in tears or in rejoicing. Cultivate the soil of my heart to believe You and to trust

You. May I be surrounded by Your grace for the journey. May it be a sacred, holy, protected, and nourished journey with You till You bring this baby forth. I pray for a supernatural deposit of faith today. May I mount up on wings of eagles. May my position be continually at the throne of grace. Release to me the songs You are singing over me in this hour. I pray for paths to be leveled beneath my feet so my ankles do not turn. Strengthen me in my innermost being. Let worship be my shield and buckler. I pray for vision of You, Jesus. Release dreams in the night watches that strengthen me. Release to me an anointing of authority as I pray and worship my way to the birth day of Your promises in my life. What You have begun, You will be faithful to complete. And nothing will thwart the promises You have written over my life. Bless me today with a tangible manifestation of Your presence and Your power as You touch my spiritual womb, in Jesus' name. Amen!

Listen to this worship song: "Come Again" by Elevation Worship and Maverick City Music featuring Brandon Lake and Chandler Moore

Day Thirty-Two

A Warrior and a King

"'Awake, awake, Deborah! Awake, awake, break out in a song!'"
-Judges 5:12a, ESV

"Now Deborah, a prophet, the wife of Lappidoth, was leading Israel at that time. She held court under the Palm of Deborah between Ramah and Bethel in the hill country of Ephraim, and the Israelites went up to her to have their disputes decided."
-Judges 4:4-5

"'Villagers in Israel would not fight; they held back until I, Deborah, arose, until I arose, a mother in Israel.'"
-Judges 5:7

"'So may all your enemies perish, O Lord! But your friends be like the sun as he rises in his might.'"
-Judges 5:31a, ESV

Feel free to read Judges 4-5 in entirety.

There are so many prophetic words coming forth from many; God is raising up Deborah's in this hour. It's a glorious and beautiful word coming from the throne room of Heaven. Nate and Christy Johnson proclaimed, "I can hear the sound of a great and mighty army marching on the horizon. It is an army of God's daughters, coming to claim their inheritance. I can feel the ground shaking as they march together in unison, sending shockwaves into the enemy's camp for they come to retrieve their territory."

Sister, before we pick up any mantle, assignment, or calling, we must know foundationally that we are loved. We are chosen. We are enough because he is enough. We want to partner with the Lord to bring forth transformation, revival, and reformation, which is marvelous. But if we don't move out in our calling in the understanding of our identity of being loved daughters of God, we can lose sight of who we really are in the midst of the work. (Father, release to us a revelation of Your love for us and the depth of our identity as daughters.) We have to know this at a bone-deep level, daughters of the Most High God. He must release this insight and understanding to us in greater revelation and conviction in this hour.

We are not just workers; we are daughters!

Deborah, this warrior woman of deep intimacy with God, came on the scene during decades of oppression. The enemy was ensnaring God's people. They were wayward once again, tantalized by false gods and living out of that belief system. It was time for repentance and returning. (It took them about 20 years of living in misery before they finally cried out to God.) The Israelites, under Canaanite rule, were disarmed and unable to fight. Public roads were unsafe for travel, and there was much anarchy and confusion released in the land. I would say they were in a "lockdown" of sorts. How that sounds like 2020.

God found a willing woman to bring forth victory for His people. She was a wife and a mother. She knew her God from her place as intercessor and prophet (both requiring deep intimacy with the Lord). She was also a judge and military strategist who led her nation to freedom and victory. She called her nation back to righteousness, knowing the times and seasons that were appointed both for her and the people of God—thanks to those princes of Issachar who were with her (Judges 5:15). I would say based on all this, Deborah brought forth revival to Israel first from her place of intimacy with her Father and then with a movement of faith, vision, and courage. You don't have one without the other.

> "As the Lord begins to direct you to embrace your calling and the stirring in your heart for His destiny and purpose for you, I believe that you will begin to take on a similar divine urgency and sense of responsibility for things greater than yourself. I believe that you will begin to see yourself as a woman of influence, conviction, and power. There is a divinely inspired cry coming out of your spirit, declaring, 'Not on my watch!' The passion and righteous indignation of the Lord is arising in the hearts of women to take up the sword of the Spirit to touch heaven through prayer and intercession to bring reformation on the earth." -Michelle McClain-Walters[22]

Deborah was not afraid to confront the enemy. She was not afraid to rally the armies of Israelites and move with the word of the Lord and the strategies of Heaven. She didn't fear man, but she feared God. She wanted freedom and repentance for her nation. I believe the justice of God pulsated through her veins. She was one who released the prophetic words to God's people as both an intercessor, judge, and prophet. She didn't question what she received, but she moved on with courage and boldness, clarity and vision. She did not back down or back out. She arose as a mother in Israel with persistence and authority and power. As I write this and know many of your stories, I declare to you: He's doing the exact same thing with you today in your areas of leadership and influence. But hear me on this: our intimacy with the Lord is imperative before we take one step to the right or the left. If you don't have the yes of the Lord, do not move, even if the idea or offer seems to fall right in line with your gifting and calling. And with that, fear and confusion have no place to counsel or minister to you as you listen for the Holy Spirit to speak.

One of the most glorious aspects of Deborah's life is that she was a worshipper. In Judges 5 she sings a song of worship, retelling the story and giving the glory to God and God alone. This was her greatest weapon. She could mobilize armies with the strategies of Heaven, but I believe her worship was the drum beat of her life. Why? Because this was the very thing that generations could sing with her. Thousands and thousands of years later, we are still reading her song of worship.

Worship moves the heart of God and transforms nations and generations.

Sister, neighborhoods, cities, and nations are awaiting your intercession, worship, and words to prophesy them into their fulfillment and restoration. The armies of Heaven are waiting for you to put them on assignment as God gives you the word. Can you even fathom that? When my oldest daughter, Lizzy, was around 15 years of age, there was a couple praying for her, and the husband prophesied over her, "Your worship will put angels on assignment!" I believe wholeheartedly that, as a worship leader, she brings Heaven to Earth and angels move in their callings and assignments. It's time to take your place under the Palm of Deborah (signifying providence and wisdom from the Lord) and awake and arise to your place.

**Nations and generations are waiting for your voice
to come forth as Jesus longs to release His freedom
and victory right through your mouth.**

Deborah had to have an awakening moment. There was a time in her life when God said to her, *"Awake, awake, Deborah (Judges 5:12a)!"* There was a time when she must have said, "Yes," to the Lord to begin to step into all God had for her. I doubt she laid under that palm and sunbathed and read magazines hoping to one day step into her destiny. If she was a judge who knew the times and seasons, God obviously had training and learning for her in preparation. The process for Deborah's profound leadership mattered to God. All the days before she stepped onto the scene as judge and prophet and intercessor and worshipper and warrior mattered to the Lord. Her years and years of preparation mattered to the Lord, and He used every ounce of it to bring victory to her nation and to the people of Israel on the matters that conflicted them. Please hear me: God is in these days of mundane, hard, tumultuous, lonely, joyful, in-over-your-head, overwhelming, and underwhelming. And all of it is preparing you to be raised as a spiritual mother in your nation so you know how to steward well all He hands to you.

> **Your lifestyle of passionately pursuing Jesus is going to call scores of people to return to their first love as well as come alive to Him for the very first time.**

"So I say to you young ladies, use your God-given abilities. You have the power to leave your mark on the world, to make a difference. From the stay at home mom, to the woman in government, you are extremely important. Let your fingerprints be on the next great breakthrough, an innovative creation, or perhaps the cure for cancer. As moms, or even a great teacher, shape the lives and minds of children, who will be the next history makers. Be one who helps strengthen our nation, or even the world, and represents well the One whom we serve—King Jesus." -Dutch Sheets[23]

When Jesus awakened your heart to Him, you were dressed in new robes, and your tree of victory was the cross. And He made a massive deposit in your life when He decided to come wash you by His blood and dwell in you by His Spirit. That way you could move in power and hear Him clearly. We are even better equipped than Deborah was—we have the cross, and we have the Spirit. What Deborah did in the Old Testament for Israel, Jesus commissions us to do for the nations. So now, as God is raising up an army of Deborahs, will you be one who raises her hand and says, "Lord, I want to carry forth that calling in Your story of redemption and revival throughout the Earth"? Will you give God your yes before He even invites you into this place of leadership? If He's wooing you right now to this place of worship and surrender, just dive in over your head. He is trustworthy, and He is good.

My prayer is that we would be part of that army of passionate Jesus lovers who count our lives as nothing but knowing Christ and Him crucified. He will fill in the rest.

> "Daughter-prophets—arise and advance! It's time for you to *arise*, embrace this calling and assignment, and it is time for you to advance. This means that you take every-day, little steps toward fulfilling this assignment. Don't despise the un-glamorous steps along the journey, for the very generation that's waiting for you is *not* looking for glamour. They don't want a spiritual show. They want authenticity. They want real. They want diapers and dis-appointment. They want to hear about the breakthrough and breakdown. They want the pure, the real." -Patricia King[24]

Let's go make history with God, together!

Listen to this worship song: "Jireh" by Elevation Worship and Maverick City Music

Day Thirty-Three

---⚜---

MY RADICAL TESTIMONY

"In those days John the Baptist came, preaching in the wilderness of Judea and saying, 'Repent, for the kingdom of heaven has come near.' This is he who was spoken of through the prophet Isaiah:

"'A voice of one calling in the wilderness, "Prepare the way for the Lord, make straight paths for him."'"

"John's clothes were made of camel's hair, and he had a leather belt around his waist. His food was locusts and wild honey."
-Matthew 3:1-4

"'Those who repent I baptize with water, but there is coming a man after me who is more powerful than I. In fact, I'm not even worthy enough to pick up his sandals. He will submerge you into union with the Spirit of Holiness and with a raging fire! He comes with a winnowing fork in his hands and comes to his threshing floor to sift what is worthless from what is pure. And he is ready to sweep out his threshing floor and gather his wheat into his granary, but the straw he will burn up with a fire that can't be extinguished!'"
-Matthew 3:11-12, TPT

The Holy Spirit dropped these words into my spirit:

> I am looking for radical lovers who will live out a radical
> testimony for all the world to see. These ones will receive
> the baptism of fire and burn for Me.

God is raising up His forerunners in this significant moment of reset. He has prepared them, and they will burn for Him. Many will encounter their radical lives of passionate pursuit and turn to God. They will be ignition points of both the demonstration and proclamation of the gospel. There will be an army of revivalists bent on the purposes of God with their gazes fixed on Him and the chains that held them to the pursuit of earthly kingdoms radically broken.

John the Baptist has always been my favorite person in Scripture, apart from Christ of course. I love his radical life of set-apartness. He was marked before the creation of the world to be a forerunner for the Messiah. He preached a revolutionary message with urgency and conviction and to prepare hearts for the coming of Jesus. He was fearless, simple in his devotion, unwavering, and passionate—the very things that are to mark us now, dear sister.

> "As a Believer, you are a walking encounter of the living
> God. You are the embodiment of God's revival." -Kris
> Vallotton

We have a testimony of the saving grace of Jesus; He has brought us from death to life. We live in a spiritual desert called the world, where Christians are becoming more and more the odd man out. Moral absolutes and absolute truth "social distance" even in the Church. More often than not you can't even tell us apart from the world. And yet there's a voice of one calling in the desert, *"Prepare the way for the Lord (Matthew 3:3)."* Do you hear the Spirit's invitation?

"In the spirit of today's age, John's ministry would have been very different. He wouldn't start in the wilderness. He wouldn't dress funny. He wouldn't preach such a straightforward message. He would use marketing surveys and focus groups to hone his message and presentation. John wasn't motivated by the spirit of today's age, but by the Spirit of God." -David Guzik, Matthew 3 commentary

Sister, we can't lose our voice or our calling to come out, be set apart, marked and moving in the power of the Holy Spirit. Where did we buy into the lie that we were supposed to blend in and shut up? God is looking for His burning ones who are purified by fire. He is touching the lips of those, just like He did with Isaiah (Isaiah 6:1-8), who will have a sanctified message and who will burn with the fire of God. He gave you His glory (*"I have given them the glory that you gave me ... (John 17:22a)."*) and it rests on you (*"... for the Spirit of glory and of God rests on you (1 Peter 4:14b)."*). He will partner with you to bring Heaven to Earth with your radical testimony and the power of His life in you. We receive salvation for free. But there will be a cost to the depth of intimacy He will invite you to go with Him. Would you allow Him to take you even deeper?

"I am asking you to make an irrevocable decision to be in the middle of God's greatest acts in history. At this moment, God is selecting people and working in them for unmatched power to overcome evil. He is recruiting people to do things that are beyond comprehension. Someone is going to heed this call and do astonishing works for Christ. I must ask ... why not you?" -Mario Murillo[25]

Johns' life was radical in order to prepare a nation for the coming Messiah. An army of passionate laid down lovers of Jesus are taking up the same calling. It's called revival, and it's happening now. It begins with surrender. Billions will hear the name of Jesus for the first time, and Heaven will be filled with the nations because many are awakening and living their lives bent on the purposes of God. He will come and fill you with the fire of unwavering passion and power, for His name's sake and for His glory. You have been marked and assigned for glory—His glory. Will you take your place in this time of revival and pick up what He has for you? Your very life will carry eternity.

If this is the desire of your heart, perhaps you want to get on your knees as you declare this prayer.

> Lord, I want to burn for You. All that I am. All You have destined for my life before the foundations of the world. May it be consumed by You, Jesus. Let me be marked by radical passion for You. May I be counted as one of Your burning ones, who is consumed with Your purposes right now. Lord, would You burn up fear of man, timidity, and people pleasing? Would You touch my lips and sanctify my tongue that I would speak the words of the Lord with boldness and resoluteness? I forsake all else, and I lay my life before You to be consumed by You, Jesus. Anoint my life, train me, prepare me, and set me ablaze for Your glory and because of Your goodness. I want to be counted as one who prepares the way for the return of Jesus to this generation and this time in history. Bring revival in me first, and then bring it through me, Lord. In Jesus' name, amen.

Listen to this worship song: "My Testimony" by Elevation Worship

Day   Thirty-Four

A LIFE LAID DOWN

"Then Jesus went back across the Jordan to the place where John had been
baptizing in the early days. There he stayed, and many people came to
him. They said, 'Though John never performed a sign, all that John said
about this man was true.' And in that place many believed in Jesus."
-John 10:40-42

"The next day, Jesus walked right past where John and two of
his disciples were standing. John, gazing upon Jesus, pointed to
him and prophesied, 'Look! There's God's sacrificial Lamb!' And
as soon as John's two disciples heard this, they immediately left
John and began to follow a short distance behind Jesus.

"Jesus turned around and saw they were following him and asked, 'What
do you want?' They responded, 'Rabbi (which means, Master Teacher),
where are you staying?' Jesus answered, 'Come and discover for yourselves.'
So they went with him and saw where he was staying, and since it
was late in the afternoon, they spent the rest of the day with Jesus."
-John 1:35-39, TPT

In the passage from John 10, Jesus takes a moment to escape opposition
and heads back to the original place where John first prepared the ground
for the coming of the Messiah. He goes back. There are some who need to
know if they should go back to the places they once planted the seeds of

the gospel. Jesus went back to fulfill what began in John's life and ministry. John couldn't finish out the great harvest of souls, but Jesus could. I think someone needs to hear these words:

Go back and finish what was once started for the sake of the gospel.

John was such a curiously passionate man. What made him live such a radical, spirit-infused life when he didn't yet know Jesus? His whole life was broken open and poured out for Jesus. He was a revivalist and a reformer, and Jesus longed to complete the work John began. Jesus' returning to that region speaks to me of honor and intentionality. I draw four compelling conclusions:

1. The places where you have declared Jesus are where He will return for harvesting.
2. Your testimony of faith and your life of radical holiness plant seeds in the lives of people. If you never perform one miracle, people still see the story of your life. Your surrendered life is a miracle to a watching world.
3. A prophet is never welcome in his hometown, but Jesus revisits that place and brings forth the harvest you planted as mere seeds.
4. All that John said about this man was true. Jesus fulfilled John's testimony. He had his "I told you so!" moment. He will have that with each of our lives.

John 1:38 is the first recorded saying of Jesus in this Gospel. He poses a question to His curious onlookers, the same question He asks every Christ follower. What do we want in following Jesus? What are we really looking for? Is it something we are seeking for ourselves, or are we willing to be radical and surrendered even if we don't see the final chapter of glory here on Earth? Do we want a ministry? A calling? A purpose? Answers to prayers we've prayed our whole lives? Or do we simply want Jesus, to be in His presence and to know Him? John's disciples asked where Jesus was staying, showing they were only seeking Him. Curiously they followed and spent the day in His presence.

Sister, you need to know that what moves your heart moves His. Where you have been hidden and faithful, He sees. The places you have lived, served, planted, and watered, Jesus will revisit. The faith and perseverance you have applied that only He knows, He will honor. He will fulfill the work you began there. When you thought no one was really listening and watching, your life was on display. And Jesus goes back and steps His feet in that place.

- He honors the places where you have ministered!
- You may go on from this place, but Jesus will revisit it!
- If God moves you from a place, He hasn't forgotten it!

I think of my dear friend, Judy, who has served the homeless in Dallas for nearly two decades, and that service recently came to an end. Her heart and life were poured out into that community. Jesus will go back there, Judy, and bring forth a harvest.

I think of Jim Elliot, who was martyred by the Aucas in attempt to bring them Jesus. It was not until Elisabeth, his wife, returned that many Aucas became Christians.

I think of my parents, who took the gospel to Turkey for nearly two decades. They fearlessly and courageously sowed and sowed. Three years ago, the Lord passed the baton to me. He will carry forth the callings to the generations that follow you.

"I could go on and on, but I've run out of time. There are so many more—Gideon, Barak, Samson, Jephthah, David, Samuel, the prophets. ... Through acts of faith, they toppled kingdoms, made justice work, took the promises for themselves. They were protected from lions, fires, and sword thrusts, turned disadvantage to advantage, won battles, routed

alien armies. Women received their loved ones back from the dead. There were those who, under torture, refused to give in and go free, preferring something better: resurrection. Others braved abuse and whips, and, yes, chains and dungeons. We have stories of those who were stoned, sawed in two, murdered in cold blood; stories of vagrants wandering the earth in animal skins, homeless, friendless, powerless—the world didn't deserve them!—making their way as best they could on the cruel edges of the world.

"Not one of these people, even though their lives of faith were exemplary, got their hands on what was promised. God had a better plan for us: that their faith and our faith would come together to make one completed whole, their lives of faith not complete apart from ours."
-Hebrews 11:32-40, MSG

John never saw the fulfillment of his entire calling. He prepared the way of the Lord, but I'm sure he wasn't ready to be snuffed out so quickly when Jesus came on the scene. But Jesus goes back to our callings, and He personally shows up and brings fulfillment. To those of you whose ministries seem to have ended because of sickness, Jesus will go back. To those of you who experienced the tragedy of the loss of your spouse, Jesus will carry your calling forth with Him as your Bridegroom beside you. To those of you who seem to have lost the battle over what God called you to, you better believe He's speaking His final word of victory over it. He has the last word on that battle!

Let me close with a part of a prophetic word from Lana Vawser from December 2020:

> "I began to see daughters of God all over the world beginning to receive the manifestation of that which the Lord has spoken to them. They were moving from hope deferred to hope assured. They were moving from discouragement to joy. From despair to dreaming again.

The Lord is breathing refreshing hope and life over many daughters right now. The long-awaited promises are manifesting now. I heard many daughters of God crying out 'I have waited my whole life for this'. The faithfulness of God resounded loudly around me as I watched daughters of God falling on their knees weeping and weeping in joy and thankfulness to the Lord that He has fulfilled that which He has spoken and that which He had promised."[26]

Let me pray for us.

Lord, take us to a whole new level of surrender. No matter if we see the justice or the fulfillment of the promise or the answer to a certain prayer, may we pour it all out on You. I pray that we would live with the radical surrender of John the Baptist, with the volume and declaration, "Prepare the way of the Lord!" I pray for hope deferred, that You would go back and walk that ground and bring forth harvest from abandoned places. I pray for those prophets who are not welcomed in their own homelands, that You would lead them to new places of welcome and receptivity so their giftings can explode. I pray for favor on the heads of my sisters so they not only walk about in peace, but so they walk about in worship. Take hold of every empty place that needs to be filled with Your presence and overflow. I pray for my sisters to carry a new fire; consume them, Jesus, with all that You are. They will be marked forever, no matter what the past tries to define over them. I pray that shame and sadness and disappointment and grief would be the offering they break before You and pour on Your feet. Receive it as worship, Jesus. And in turn use it to anoint their feet with the gospel of peace for nations and generations. In the mighty name of Jesus, amen!

Listen to this worship song: "Move Your Heart" by Maverick City Music and Upperroom

Day Thirty-Five

BARREN NO MORE

*"'I will open up refreshing streams on the barren hills and
springing fountains in the valleys. I will make the desert a
pleasant pool and the dry land springs of water.'"*
-Isaiah 41:18, TPT

*"Even when their paths wind through the dark valley of tears, they
dig deep to find a pleasant pool where others find only pain. He gives
to them a brook of blessing filled from the rain of an outpouring."*
-Psalm 84:6, TPT

Receive these promises from God's Word today. Look at your places of barrenness, wilderness, suffering, and regret and see what God is going to do in and through you. I believe it with all my heart. He's doing a new thing.

I must give testimony to the One who brings forth life in barren seasons and barren wombs. I receive stories of the hand of God moving in the lives of women as He stirs and brings forth life in wilderness places. I don't know if there is anything more gloriously celebratory to me than when women come alive with fresh passion and faith and who burn with the fire of God, in spite of what life has thrown them. I will give my zeal, my energy, my heart to see this come forth because I believe we are in a time in history when Heaven is moving in acceleration to see women arise in their calling, to be reset, restored, and renewed so they can be carriers of

REVIVALIST ARISE ❦ 171

revival. Jesus was the leader of the first women's liberation movement, and don't think for a second His heart has changed on the matter.

One of my best friends, Leslie, has had several pregnancy dreams. One night both of us had a dream of her having a baby. God is speaking to her and making her ready to carry His purposes forth. So much of what we will carry forward has been because we have walked through the valley of the shadow of death in past seasons. He has made us ready for this new era that is going to require the faith that was deposited from fiery trials and lions' dens of past seasons. You don't learn how to wage war by being sheltered from every trial and temptation. You wage war because He has personally taught your hand to bend a bow, chase a lion, tend sheep, and take the sword of the enemy and cut his head off.

Sister, I declare to you today: the past places of pain and heartache are going to be the very places of anointing and authority for you. Redemption is coming. You will have a testimony to bring to a hopeless and dying world. You will have the words of victory and healing you wept in the dark night of the soul and declare over someone else for their breakthrough. Nothing will be wasted. Hear me on this: God will use every drop from past seasons for what He is bringing forth in you right now.

I am walking with a dear friend in her own place of revival. I am watching God rescue, redeem, and restore her life and ultimately her calling to greater expanse. He is setting her feet on higher ground. It's quite something to perceive the calling on another's life and watch the hand of God tethering her to Himself to get her ready for increase. We need people who "see" the calling on our lives and call us forth into even deeper waters. We need those who have been in the ditch to have the words to call us up.

We cannot lead others where we ourselves have not walked.

"But the Lord said to Samuel, 'Do not consider his appearance or his height, for I have rejected him. The Lord does not look at the things people look at. People look at the outward appearance, but the Lord looks at the heart.'"
-1 Samuel 16:7

"When the angel of the Lord appeared to Gideon, he said, 'The Lord is with you, mighty warrior.'"
-Judges 6:12

David didn't see himself as a king, but God declared it. Gideon didn't see himself as a mighty warrior as he was hiding in a wine press, but God saw that in him and declared it. If the Lord were standing before you, what would He call you today? Champion, victorious one, righteous, warrior, holy, pure, blameless, fearless, marked and called one, mighty woman of valor, freedom fighter? I believe He would look at you and say all these things because that is who He is inside you. He is living His life and His identity inside your surrendered life. What God has declared over your life, He will be faithful to fulfill with exponentially more than what you envision. And He will go back, and all the things from past seasons will be marked by Him for His glory, redemption, victory, and harvest.

So based on that truth, let's go back to those barren places where you have longed to see life come forth. Let's go back and speak to the wilderness or the field of dry bones and declare to that thing that it's time for life to come forth. We go in our identity of Christ in us, full of the Spirit of God who moves with resurrection power, surrounded by the love of the Father and our identity as a daughter and with the authority of Christ. We can see what He sees and speak His powerful Word over people, places, and situations. Nothing is untouchable when Jesus comes.

"Then on the most important day of the feast, the last day, Jesus stood and shouted out to the crowds—'All you thirsty ones, come to me! Come to me

and drink! Believe in me so that rivers of living water will burst out from
within you, flowing from your innermost being, just like the Scripture says!'"
-John 7:37-38, TPT

Rivers will flow from your innermost being because Jesus said they would. Period. They will overflow to people and cities and nations who have been longing to swim in the ocean of His goodness and never knew. We live surrendered, and the waters begin to flow. Thirsty people will begin to come to you for water as you allow those rivers to flow. And this is what it will look like:

"The wilderness and dry land will be joyously glad! The desert will blossom
like a rose and rejoice! Every dry and barren place will burst forth with
abundant blossoms, dancing and spinning with delight! Lebanon's lush
splendor covers it, the magnificent beauty of Carmel and Sharon. My people
will see the awesome glory of Yahweh, the beautiful grandeur of our God.
Strengthen those who are discouraged. Energize those who feel defeated. Say
to the anxious and fearful, 'Be strong and never afraid. Look, here comes
your God! He is breaking through to give you victory! He comes to avenge
your enemies. With divine retribution he comes to save you!' Then blind eyes
will open and deaf ears will hear. Then the lame will leap like playful deer
and the tongue-tied will sing songs of triumph. Gushing water will spring
up in the wilderness and streams will flow through the desert. The burning
sand will become a refreshing oasis, the parched ground bubbling springs,
and the dragon's lair a meadow with grass, reeds, and papyrus. There will
be a highway of holiness called the Sacred Way. The impure will not be
permitted on this road, but it will be accessible to God's people. And not
even fools will lose their way. The lion will not be found there; no wild beast
will travel on it—they will not be found there. But the redeemed will find
a pathway on it. Yahweh's ransomed ones will return with glee to Zion.
They will enter with a song of rejoicing and be crowned with everlasting
joy. Ecstatic joy will overwhelm them; weariness and grief will disappear!"
-Isaiah 35:1-10, TPT

Beloved, would you dare to position yourself at the feet of Jesus today and ask Him to increase the flow of the river coming forth from your life? Would you dare to ask Him to take you to places of even greater surrender so that Christ, who is your very life, would flow out and water barren, searching lives all around you? Would you position yourself to receive His overflow and let it burst forth from inside of you? I bless you today in the powerful and mighty name of Jesus.

Listen to this worship song: "New Thing" by Red Rocks Worship

THE CONSECRATED ONES: FOR HIS GLORY AND HIS HARVEST

"He replied to them, 'Now is the time for the Son of Man to be glorified. Let me make this clear: A single grain of wheat will never be more than a single grain of wheat unless it drops into the ground and dies. Because then it sprouts and produces a great harvest of wheat—all because one grain died.

"'The person who loves his life and pampers himself will miss true life! But the one who detaches his life from this world and abandons himself to me, will find true life and enjoy it forever! If you want to be my disciple, follow me and you will go where I am going. And if you truly follow me as my disciple, the Father will shower his favor upon your life.

"'Even though I am torn within, and my soul is in turmoil, I will not ask the Father to rescue me from this hour of trial. For I have come to fulfill my purpose—to offer myself to God. So, Father, bring glory to your name!' Then suddenly a booming voice was heard from the sky,

"'I have glorified my name! And I will glorify it through you again!'

"The audible voice of God startled the crowd standing nearby. Some thought it was only thunder, yet others said, 'An angel just spoke to him!'

"Then Jesus told them, 'The voice you heard was not for my benefit, but for yours—to help you believe.'"
-John 12:23-30, TPT

Jesus had quite the prophetic celebration as He entered Jerusalem. The people were declaring His kingship and His salvation, even though they had no idea what this meant. Earlier that morning, Jesus wept over the city because they had missed him. Many had completely disregarded His coming. How He longed for them to really know Him and to know His heart for all mankind. I can't even imagine the vast territory of emotion Jesus must have scoured as He entered the first day of the last week of His life. I wonder if His heart was overwhelmed with a fresh gift of love deposited by the Father for those He was about to die for (Romans 5:5). Was it this love that evoked tears for all those who would miss Him? Was it this love that allowed Him to see the glorious Bride that would be handed to Him after the cross? I believe it was you, the very joy set before Him, that kept His feet walking.

Father God speaks up for a third time in Jesus' life. First, we hear His identity at His baptism (Matthew 3:16-17). The second time, the Father speaks of Jesus' authority (Matthew 17:5). Now this time, His Father calls attention to His authentication and vision for all of Christ's earthly life—His glory! Everything Jesus did pointed to the glory of the Father. He glorified Him continually through His life, and He would do it again, and this time it would be a final glorification. And then He would place this glory in us.

> Oh, Jesus, that You would want me, with all my frailties and inadequacies. You take this fragile life, and You will manifest Your glorious life through it. This is hard for me to completely fathom. You found me and decided at Your first glimpse that You would put Your glory on me, and together, Your life inside of my life would bring Yourself glory. How is that, Lord?

Jesus said in John 17:10, *"And glory has come to me through them.'"* It was in the Father's perfect plan to bring forth a Bride for His Son that would be the image bearer of His glory.

> "Behold the towering passion of your God: The Church, the *ekklesia*, is His ultimate passion. She is His central thought. She is His eternal purpose. This glorious woman is in Him, by Him, through Him, and to Him. God's grand mission is to obtain a bride who passionately loves His Son." -Frank Viola[27]

What I find so poignant in this passage is how the words of Jesus regarding the "harvest" are in direct relation to the glory of Jesus. The two are so beautifully connected.

The great harvest of souls from the world He so loves is in direct relationship to God's glory. There will not be one without the other.

I have sensed, as many have been praying for a massive harvest of souls for generations, that He's ready to pour revival out. I feel the stirring of the release of what is currently upon us in spite of turmoil and transition. I am seeing this take place in a two-fold manner: the Bride awakening to this overcoming love for her Jesus and the lost coming to salvation in droves! It is happening right now, before our very eyes.

As I sat with the Lord, I sensed His precious counsel in my spirit, I began to pend these words:

> A righteous remnant is being called up, consecrated, and prepared for these last days. When confronted, many "believers" will say nothing. They will keep quiet so as to not rock the boat. But the remnant will lead the Church. The remnant will arise with boldness and with a voice. Their

voice will help to draw the line between those who are with God and those who are not. I will anoint My consecrated ones to leadership with courage and boldness. They will not meld into culture but will be outcasts in many ways—a John the Baptist anointing to prepare the way of the Lord. These ones will be called up in this hour. They will not desire fame or recognition. They will not want the limelight. They will follow Me with passion and abandon because I will be their everything. Even in the loss of family and friends, I will satisfy them with Myself so they will not even consider the loss. I will take hold of them and lead them and satisfy them. My consecrated ones belong to Me. And no one will snatch them from My hand. They will be so undone with My wonder, My words, and My presence that they will be satisfied, content, and full. And these will lead the many to Me.

"This is your season that you will leave the sidelines and join the frontlines." -Nate Johnson

One of my dearest friends, Stacy, is a living testimony of this very thing. I met her on my first all-women's trip to the Middle East. We were headed to a country that is 99% Muslim and very intimidating when it comes to sharing the gospel. But that is why we were there. I can recap the entire 10 days in just a few words: it was the hardest trip for Stacy. She was overwhelmed and disenchanted with the whole thing. But in the midst of the tension and culture shock, something was happening; her heart was awakening to being loved by the Beloved. She came home, and this persistent wooing of Jesus has not stopped. She has since gone with me to Latin America and Austin, and the Lord redeemed every detail and then some as scores of people said, "Yes," to Jesus through her surrendered life. I am watching a woman being transformed by the divine romance of her Bridegroom. She has been a living picture of what Jesus wants to do to get His harvesters prepared, ready, waiting, and moving. And now she is coming on staff with East-West to help me build and expand this Arise movement.

> *"And we all, who with unveiled faces contemplate the Lord's glory, are being transformed into his image with ever-increasing glory, which comes from the Lord, who is the Spirit."*
> -2 Corinthians 3:18

A harvest will take place because of the cross. A harvest will declare the glory of God. Nations will come to Him. Generations will be drawn to this Jesus. But for this to have happened, His life must be broken and presumably fall to the ground and break open. Earth was not worthy of this precious life. But He did it so an invitation of salvation could reverberate across the globe to places unreached. Today, His invitation to be a harvester hangs in the balance. If we indeed bear the ever-increasing glory of God and His heart is for the world to know Him, we can't skip over this divine moment and God's booming words. He is *"encouraging, comforting and urging you to live lives worthy of God, who calls you into his kingdom and glory (1 Thessalonians 2:12)."*

We weren't meant to hear the Father's stamp of glory on the Son and dismiss our identity in that very statement because that glory is part of our identity now. That word of harvest is part of our life's mission because it's the mission of Christ in you.

> *"'Who will not fear you, Lord, and bring glory to your name? For you alone are holy. All nations will come and worship before you, for your righteous acts have been revealed.'"*
> -Revelation 15:4

As you listen to the worship song today, make it your prayer. His fire will fall on His consecrated ones. He will set you aflame for His glory and for

His harvest. And together we will go find the remnant of women who are coming to the front lines. The Lord is raising up an army of people who will carry the fire of God and shift history, cities, and entire families for eternity. In Jesus' name, do it, Lord.

Listen to this worship song: "Living Sacrifice" by Brandon Lake

Day Thirty-Seven

IMMOVABLE RESOLVE

"From Peter, an apostle of Jesus the Anointed One, to the chosen ones who have been scattered like 'seed' into the nations living as refugees, in Pontus, Galatia, Cappadocia, and throughout the Roman provinces of Asia and Bithynia. You are not forgotten, for you have been chosen and destined by Father God. The Holy Spirit has set you apart to be God's holy ones, obedient followers of Jesus Christ who have been gloriously sprinkled with his blood. May God's delightful grace and peace cascade over you many times over!"
-1 Peter 1:1-2, TPT

Peter, the one man mentioned second to Jesus in the Gospels. He's a man whose life consisted of failure and zeal, unbridled courage, victory, fear, and great faith. He knew what cost looked like, and he knew the pain and need to be reinstated by Jesus. His past didn't define his calling, but it sure shaped it. Grace became the foundation of Peter's life. And in the midst of persecution and suffering, he called this baby church to even more, no matter the cost.

On the shores of Galilee as a young fisherman, Peter was called by Jesus to begin a life of impossibility. He was then commissioned on the beach by Jesus in Luke 22:32, TPT: *"But I have prayed for you, Peter, that you would stay faithful to me no matter what comes. Remember this: after you have turned back to me and have been restored, make it your life mission to strengthen the faith of your brothers.'"* At Pentecost, 3,000 people were saved as the words of Christ were declared through Peter's lips. In partnership with the power of the Spirit, this man turned the world upside down. And historians record that he was even crucified upside down on a cross.

He carried the gospel power, wrapped in the reformational message of grace to the places God assigned for him. He held back once and never did it again. His life was marked for the sake of the gospel to the very end.

Read 1 Peter 1:1-9 to see what we have been given in Christ:

- We are the chosen and destined ones of God.
- We are temporary residents in a foreign land.
- We are set apart as His Holy ones; holiness is our inheritance.
- He had foreknowledge of us, enwrapped in His omniscience, fully known.
- We are gloriously covered by His blood and made clean.
- Grace and peace is ours for the taking!
- We have extravagant mercy for this journey called life.
- We have a new, living, energetic, extravagant hope.
- We have been reborn and given an incorruptible inheritance that is eternal.
- We are kept by the power of God, and our salvation is secure.
- He has given us the gift of faith to hold onto until Jesus comes.

These things are true of us, and yet trial will come. Your faith will be tested as you go because it is so precious to the Lord.

> "Our faith isn't tested because God doesn't know how much or what kind of faith we have. It is tested because we often are ignorant of how much or what kind of faith we have. God's purpose in testing is to display the enduring quality of our faith. ... If gold is fit to be tested and

purified by fire, then how much more our faith, which is far more precious than gold? God has a great and important purpose in testing our faith." -David Guzik

Peter could go back and strengthen the church because of what he walked through. He could call up the faith of that infant church because he knew the grace and mercy and love of Jesus so deep inside himself. There was a resolute conviction in his bones that he testifies to in the pages of his letters.

I remember a time when I metaphorically took my shoes off in following Jesus. I was disillusioned, distraught, and foundationally questioning the love of God because I couldn't see His hands of mercy in my pain. And it was not long after I knew I was being called by the Lord to radical faith when the testing came.

One December, we were on a snowy, desolate road in Oregon heading to a sledding hill. The girls were little, and we had faced one delay after another just to get on the road that morning. At every turn we were detoured no matter what we did. As we were driving, the snow began to fall and the road required snow chains for us to proceed. We pulled up behind another driver who had also stopped to put chains on his tires. My husband, Mike, got out of the van and began speaking to the man from the other car.

As I looked up, I saw my dear friend, Melissa, running to my car. She was my roommate in Santa Barbara during my senior year of college. She had endured a lot in her life, and we had lost touch for some time. I looked at her face and knew that God had miraculously and intimately moved Heaven and Earth that day for me to see and be embraced by Melissa. I knew that if God cared that much about the details of my life on that day, on that random road in Oregon, when we had traveled from Texas and she had come from California, I could trust Him.

The next morning, I remember telling the Lord I would get my shoes back on and I would follow Him no matter what. I decided in my heart and in my will that He was trustworthy, no matter the depth of my faith being tested.

**What I thought was delay became an encounter
with the intimate love of Jesus.**

Peter had a choice to take his boat back out and take up fishing after Jesus left, persecution ensued, and the believers were emotionally on the fritz. He could return to what he knew, and I presume Jesus would call and commission someone else. But Peter was so compelled by the love of God that he was willing to risk it all for the sake of the gospel. Jesus was worth the persecution. Jesus was worth the sacrifice. Jesus was worth Peter's very life. Do we have the same level of conviction?

Are we wrapped tightly enough in our identity as daughters, called ones, chosen ones, commissioned ones, marked and sealed ones? There's a burning in my heart for us to live out the rest of our days so utterly convinced of His love that come persecution, suffering, rejection from friends, etc., we are immovable in the love of God, burning for Him, until He comes for us.

That's revival. This is jubilee.

> "Everything about God is extreme in the best possible sense. He is infinitely good, infinitely holy and powerful, infinitely beautiful, magnificent, and glorious. These are just a few terms to describe Him. But none of the endless lists of traits and characteristics confine Him. Religion, which I define as form without power, tends to attempt the impossible task of restricting Him into neat little packages, giving us a false sense of intelligence and ultimately control. But He is bigger and bigger and bigger still. Each

virtue gives us a glimpse into that which is beyond measure but is open for observation. You could take one trait and explore it for all of eternity but not come close to exhausting the depths of who He is in that particular virtue." -Bill Johnson[28]

If your faith is being tested right now, I want to pray a prayer of immovable resolve over you.

> Father, I pray that in Your infinite goodness and intimate power, You would fortify my sister. I pray that, like Peter, she would overflow with conviction, by the power of the Holy Spirit, to love You passionately, no matter what it costs. I pray she would be anchored in Your love, tethered so tightly to Your heart, and operating with the mind of Christ, that each test becomes a confirmation of Your goodness. Each place of faith that is refined in the fire will bear forth the glory of God in her life. I declare that in Jesus' name. I pray for strength and steadfast immovability in her innermost being today, Lord. And I pray that joy would come in the morning—the joy of the Lord that is her strength. Fill her mouth with praise and her eyes with seeing Your hand moving things on her behalf. I pray for the gift of faith to increase, not decrease in this season, in the name of Jesus. Amen.

Listen to this worship song: "Jubilee" by Maverick City Music featuring Naomi Raine and Bryan and Katie Torwalt

Day Thirty-Eight

---❦---

IT'S TIME. LET'S GO!

"He said to them, 'Go into all the world and preach the gospel to all creation. Whoever believes and is baptized will be saved, but whoever does not believe will be condemned. And these signs will accompany those who believe: In my name they will drive out demons; they will speak in new tongues; they will pick up snakes with their hands; and when they drink deadly poison, it will not hurt them at all; they will place their hands on sick people, and they will get well.'

"After the Lord Jesus had spoken to them, he was taken up into heaven and he sat at the right hand of God. Then the disciples went out and preached everywhere, and the Lord worked with them and confirmed his word by the signs that accompanied it."
-Mark 16:15-20

Can you imagine if daily those "signs" were manifested in our lives? I think I often default to a comfort zone of the unreached mountains in South Asia where no one has heard the name Jesus. But what does it look like in a pandemic when people are sick, distressed, distraught, and financially ravaged? What does it look like to head into the grocery store and let our lives be a display of Heaven? The Lord, who had just ascended, left His team of disciples with the Holy Spirit and worked with them to put His power on display to a skeptical and desperate world. I love the language of that partnership! I love that now word for us! They came out of their quarantine of hiding and released revival!

> "We shouldn't wait around expecting that God will change us into someone we're not before He uses us. We have a tendency to say, 'God, if you'll anoint me, I'll go.' God says, 'If you'll go, I'll anoint you.' His plan is to use who we already are—the same people He made us in the first place, with the same personalities, giftings and weaknesses. Just be you. God wants to work through you and me. We aren't the main act—God is. But He's made us a crucial part of the breaking in of His kingdom." -Robby Dawkins[29]

Beloved, Jesus didn't die and commission us to go so that we would be safe and without trials, comfortable and sidelined. He died so we would be free, bold, victorious, and carry His glory. I think we have settled for and believed in a kind of comfort gospel that has lulled the Bride to sleep. In this hour we are being awakened to the truest gospel—the power, signs, wonders, miracles, and reality of the cross and resurrection—for the love of the world Jesus died for.

I wish I could look you in the eyes and say with all my heart, "You have been made ready for this moment!" God has made you ready. It's time to awaken to the destiny He has spoken over your life—the plans and purposes He has spoken. It's time to throw off everything that entangles us and run with passion. What if we lost it all for the sake of Jesus! What if the anthem of our lives became, *"For to me, to live is Christ ... (Philippians 1:21)"*? What if we dared to say to the Lord, "I hand you this fragile life, and I ask you to exchange my plans and purposes for Yours"? This is our hour of abundance, not wilderness; fruitfulness, not powerlessness.

There are places and people that have been assigned to you that no one else can touch right now.

God has given many of you the gift to heal; go fearlessly and pray for people. He has given some of you the gift to love people through hospitality.

> I pray for divine instructions to tangibly love and minister to people right now with your unique and creative expression. Intercessors, move Heaven with your faithful intercession. No one may see it, but I pray that metaphorically your knees are bruised in this hour as you kneel in the gap for so many.

> Entrepreneurs, I pray a release of creativity over you right now for new income streams that will carry many people and expand the kingdom of Heaven here on Earth. Hidden businesses that have a kingdom agenda, I prophesy that it's time to come out of hiding into the limelight.

> Doctors, nurses, scientists, pharmacists, I pray for an anointing on your mind for solutions and ideas, and new combinations of medicine for healing. May God teach how to bring both physical and spiritual healing and deliverance to people.

> To my sisters who are apostles, prophets, teachers, pastors, and evangelists, I pray for a double portion of anointing to know exactly how to pivot and move to bring the increase of His kingdom at new depths, heights, and lengths. And I pray over all of this, the fire of His Spirit to fall on you and consume you with a passionate love for Jesus and for the world He gave His life for!

To those of you are sensing a divine reset in your own heart, don't throw it off. When Jesus wept over Jerusalem because the Jews had missed Him in their unbelief, I believe we can miss Him right now. He has come to awaken us, not with a shoulder tap but with the roar of Heaven! This is our divine interruption to get us ready for the harvest ahead. He's wooing His Bride to a dance of passion and intimacy she needs right now that is a preparation for Her wedding day. I am praying your life will be marked by the opening Scripture of this day in Mark 16:15-20.

Listen to this worship song: "Prepare the Way" by Bethel Music

Day Thirty-Nine

LAUNCH OUT INTO THE DEEP

70 Women in 70 Cities

"One day as Jesus was standing by the Lake of Gennesaret, the people were crowding around him and listening to the word of God. He saw at the water's edge two boats, left there by the fishermen, who were washing their nets. He got into one of the boats, the one belonging to Simon, and asked him to put out a little from shore. Then he sat down and taught the people from the boat.

"When he had finished speaking, he said to Simon, 'Put out into deep water, and let down the nets for a catch.'

"Simon answered, 'Master, we've worked hard all night and haven't caught anything. But because you say so, I will let down the nets.'

"When they had done so, they caught such a large number of fish that their nets began to break. So they signaled their partners in the other boat to come and help them, and they came and filled both boats so full that they began to sink."
-Luke 5:1-7

I awoke in the wee hours one morning and began to pray for my husband that God would bring him people who would draw him into deeper waters.

I began to pray this for all six of us in my precious family as I have sensed this invitation to scour the depth of the vastness of who God is. This prayer began to echo in my heart for the Bride. It's time to launch into the deep. There is too much ahead for us to remain safely on the shore, merely gazing at deeper waters.

"Deep water" in Greek from this passage of Scripture is *bathos*, meaning depth, height, of the deep sea, deep, extreme, poverty, of the deep things of God.

Jesus was standing with an initial invitation of miraculous encounter for His soon-to-be disciples as well as the crowd who had gathered. In the unknown, the impossible was coming to life. It was a whole new paradigm for these fishermen and an invitation to a life of wonder and increase. He was taking a moment to catapult these guys into the extraordinary—the deep things of God. They were just ordinary guys, and on that day, a prophetic vision was declared to Peter; he would be a fisherman of people.

> *"For he and all his companions were astonished at the catch of fish they had taken, and so were James and John, the sons of Zebedee, Simon's partners. Then Jesus said to Simon, 'Don't be afraid; from now on you will fish for people.' So they pulled their boats up on shore, left everything and followed him."*
> -Luke 5:9-11

We don't get to stay in shallow waters and explore the depth of the wonder of God. It's only for those who will swim against the reasonable, safe, and vast. But it's in this place we come to know and experience Jesus where few dare to trod.

Look with me at the places in Scripture where this same word in Greek for the deep things of God is mentioned. It paints a beautiful picture of the facets of these deep waters we are invited to scour.

The depth of His love: "... *may have power, together with all the Lord's holy people, to grasp how wide and long and high and deep is the love of Christ ... (Ephesians 3:18)."*

The deep soil for seeds to grow: "*Other seeds fell on rocky ground where they did not have much soil. They sprang up quickly because the soil was not deep (Matthew 13:5, NET)."*

The deep riches of God's wisdom: "*Oh, the depth of the riches and wisdom and knowledge of God! How unsearchable are his judgments and how fathomless his ways (Romans 11:33, NET)!"*

The deep things of God: "*God has revealed these to us by the Spirit. For the Spirit searches all things, even the deep things of God (1 Corinthians 2:10, NET)."*

No depth too great for His love: "*... nor height, nor depth, nor anything else in creation will be able to separate us from the love of God in Christ Jesus our Lord (Romans 8:39, NET)."*

The overflow even in a depth of need: "*... that during a severe ordeal of suffering, their abundant joy and their extreme poverty have overflowed in the wealth of their generosity (2 Corinthians 8:2, NET)."*

Christ is always taking His people into deep waters of discovery and abundance. Faith must take the place of sight. You will want what is on the other side of the boat! I promise. You will want the catch of impossibility that defies human reasoning. You will want the vision and calling Jesus is declaring over your life and future. You can sit and debate the invitation, or you can push out into deeper waters. And the question I have for you is this: who are the ones who will be in your boat and go with you into deeper waters?

What will be required of us in the days ahead will need to be traversed with the ones God has appointed to your boat. There are fish to be caught—billions of them, actually. Cities must be reached with the gospel. Your neighbors and mine need Jesus. But we cannot do this alone. I believe this is part of the reason behind the vision of 70 cities for Arise. We need to identify and connect the women in cities all over the U.S. who have a passionate hunger for Jesus and carry His heart for the nations. There will be a unified army of women whose hearts beat in unison for the gospel and for the One whom their hearts adore.

> "Our time for taking up a fishing pole and waiting three hours to catch one fish is over. It is not a time for one or two super-anointed evangelists to dominate the work of the harvest. It is a time for us to cooperate in laying down the vast nets God has placed in our hands. We do not need to strive to the breaking point. We simply need to be hidden inside His heart and work together. God loves it when different streams of the church join in love to take in His net. I believe He is raising up an army of laid-down lovers who will each hold on to his or her part of the net in order to bring in fish by the millions." -Heidi Baker[30]

As you stand on the shore of life, will you ask the Lord with me to take us into deeper waters? Will you ask Him to show you who your deep-water dwellers are, who will scour the depth of the goodness of God and bring in the harvest with you? Let's launch out into the deep together. Let's go find the other fisher people who are standing and watching and longing for a life of passion, significance, authenticity, and adventure. God has placed 70 boats in 70 cities in vision before us. Will you push out in one of them?

> "Jesus did not make a suggestion; He made a command. And He did not order the disciples to let down their nets to try to catch fish, He ordered them to put out their nets

for a catch of fish. In other words, Jesus was issuing both a command and a promise. The command was to put out the nets. The promise was that there would be a catch. And what a catch it would be!" -Bob Deffinbaugh

Lord, I pray for Your people today. I pray for a vision of their "boat" and their "crew." I pray for an insatiable hunger for You and only You. May our appetites for the things of God change so we would not have one foot in longing for the world and one foot standing with You. Take our feet, place them in a boat, and call us into deeper waters. I pray there would be an invitation by Your Spirit as they are reading these words. I pray for vision and promise to be spoken to them by Your Spirit for this coming year. Give them faith to leave the shore and go where they have never gone before. Give them a picture of the fish and a longing for full nets in their lives. We have the boats, and we have the nets. So I pray for courage, boldness, and faith to launch out. Raise up 70 women in 70 cities to catalyze a call and connection for other women to be a powerful force for the kingdom of God in this hour. Astound us with Your wonder and extraordinary love. In the powerful and mighty name of Jesus.

"Moving into deep water requires a full commitment. It means you weigh anchor and set your sails to catch the wind. It means you leave the shallows behind—fully surrendered to the directions of the Captain." -Dr. Paul Chappell

Listen to this worship song: "Deeper Water" by Ry Cox

NOW, GO!

"My counsel for you is simple and straightforward: Just go ahead with what you've been given. You received Christ Jesus, the Master; now live him. You're deeply rooted in him. You're well constructed upon him. You know your way around the faith. Now do what you've been taught. School's out; quit studying the subject and start living it! And let your living spill over into thanksgiving."
-Colossians 2:6-7, MSG

"In the same way you received Jesus our Lord and Messiah by faith, continue your journey of faith, progressing further into your union with him! Your spiritual roots go deeply into his life as you are continually infused with strength, encouraged in every way. For you are established in the faith you have absorbed and enriched by your devotion to him!"
-Colossians 2:6-7, TPT

Beloved, we have traversed 40 days together in the secret place with Jesus, being established and built up in the faith. We have worshipped and joined our voices in intercession with the great cloud of witnesses. We have run boldly before the throne of grace with confidence for healing, deliverance, revival, and for the hand of God to move across the Earth. We have pleaded for prodigals and for nations. We have believed and worshipped for breakthrough for us and our loved ones. We have stood in the finished work of Christ and in our identity as daughters.

An army of passionate Jesus-lovers has arisen, ready to face the weeks, months, and years ahead. We have the Word of the Lord deposited in us. Our mouths are filled with praise, and our eyes are fixed on Jesus. Now what?

Now is when we take up our sword in the Spirit and we move forward with faith. We go into the harvest field, burning with the fire of the Spirit, lamps filled with oil. When the days get darker and the world stands in hostility toward the Church, what happens? The church advances, and the people of God flourish. These days of preparation in the secret place with Jesus are for your rooting and grounding. But they are also for your advancement. Now, go!

"Every believer was faithfully devoted to following the teachings of the apostles. Their hearts were mutually linked to one another, sharing communion and coming together regularly for prayer. A deep sense of holy awe swept over everyone, and the apostles performed many miraculous signs and wonders. All the believers were in fellowship as one body, and they shared with one another whatever they had. Out of generosity they even sold their assets to distribute the proceeds to those who were in need among them. Daily they met together in the temple courts and in one another's homes to celebrate communion. They shared meals together with joyful hearts and tender humility. They were continually filled with praises to God, enjoying the favor of all the people. And the Lord kept adding to their number daily those who were coming to life."
-Acts 2:42-47, TPT

Jesus left this infant Church with a very great and grand commission to go and make disciples everywhere. And this passage from Acts is what it looked like. He breathed on them the Holy Spirit and marked and sealed them. They bore the very name of Christ, and in one day the infant church went from 120 to more than 3,000. It was harvest day in Jerusalem. Then suddenly, persecution came, and the baby Church is scattered. But they had a template for discipleship and knew what was needed to endure: Christ in them and life with one another.

You cannot live a moment without Jesus for the days ahead. You also need other women whose lamps are filled with oil, who live with the declaration, *"For to me, to live is Christ … (Philippians 1:21)."*

We need one another. We can be women whose lives look like the above passage in Acts. We can see more months of devotion, communion, worship, prayer, and life in the Spirit continually until we see Jesus face-to-face. Oh, the glorious army of women who are ablaze with the power and presence of God for the purposes of God. Come hell or high water, we know whom we have believed, and we will live for that day. Are you in? Let's go.

I want to commission you to a life of passionate pursuit of Jesus for your remaining days.

> Lord Jesus, I praise You for these 40 days of preparation and intercession. Thank You for Your clear calling to step into this journey. I pray now for the fire of Your Spirit to breathe new life, new vision, new relationships, new calling, new purpose, new territories, new hope, new passion, new boldness, and new connections.

> Commission us by Your Spirit into our realms of current influence, greater influence, and new territories that are on the way. I pray for eyes to see what and who You see. I pray for courage and boldness to run to the harvest fields and bring the kingdom of Heaven to a lost and dying world. I pray for women who will live for You and die to the lures and passions of the world. I pray for an army of women who will invade their generation for the sake of the gospel.

Place in their hands a sword, Lord Jesus, that will be wielded for Your glory. Place in their mouths the Word of God and songs of deliverance. I pray for the gifts of the Spirit to be released, that signs and wonders and miracles would follow them. Release the gift of faith and a calling to deeper intercession, in Jesus' name. Cover them with a garment of praise and joy, that they would laugh at the days to come. Be a wall of fire around them.

And I pray for 70 women who will have vision to rally other women in their communities to run passionately after Jesus. Lord, as they begin to move and transition, give them grace for change. Release dreams and visions in this next season that help to illuminate exactly where You are taking them. Lord, give them direction, clarity, and vision for the days ahead. Raise up Your daughters to be right in step with the Spirit, to hear the voice of their Savior and move with boldness and courage. Just like Joan of Arc, may they say, "I am not afraid; I was made for this!" Open the storehouses of Heaven and pour out everything they need as they hide in You, the Lover of their souls and shelter in the storm. I pray fresh anointing over their leadership, ministries, jobs, marriages, parenting, and realms of influence. Increase and expand them as they follow You, Jesus.

I pray, too, for the women who will begin house churches; give them vision and divine connections, in Jesus' name. I pray that we would lock arms in the harvest field to see the nations of the world find You, Jesus. May Heaven be filled with people because of these ones in this hour of history. Take our days and multiply them for the sake of the gospel. In the glorious and powerful name of Jesus, amen!

Listen to these worship songs as you linger a little longer: "Gold" by Jesus Culture, "Make Room" by Community Music, "Battle Belongs" by Phil Wickham

Now, go!

ABOUT THE AUTHOR

Julie King has been married to Michael for 26 years. They have had the privilege of watching their four daughters—Elizabeth, Emily, AnnMarie, and Grace—grow and develop a passion for Jesus and have a heart for the nations. Her family is the delight of her life.

Julie grew up as a missionary kid to parents who served on staff with Cru for 33 years. Much of her youth was spent living overseas in Germany, during the fall of the Berlin Wall and the opening of the Iron Curtain. It was a formative period for both her worldview and passion for the gospel. Today, Julie leads women around the world to take the gospel to people who have never heard the name of Jesus.

As an adult, Julie's desire and passion for the Bride of Christ and the lost—those who don't know Jesus personally—compelled her to begin a neighborhood Bible study to engage others in the Word and on mission. One result of this initiative was a prayer and worship gathering in Frisco, Texas, called God of the City: The Church unified-revived-unleashed. This three-year planting of the Lord was a movement to unite the church in North Dallas for the purpose of worship and prayer for revival. Hundreds of churches participated in the event, which was attended by thousands of people.

In 2018, Julie began an initiative called Arise through the mission of East-West. Through this effort, she is seeing women grow in a depth of hunger and passion for Jesus and His heart for the world. Julie serves as a full-time missionary with East-West.

Julie has a passion for the Word and for worship and loves rallying people to the very things God brings forth in her spirit. This book is a result of those passions, and she believes there's more to come.

ABOUT EAST-WEST

East-West began because two men couldn't resist the call of Christ's great mission: go into the world and make disciples (Matthew 28:18-20).

Through their work behind the Iron Curtain in the early 1980s, East-West founders, John Maisel and Bud Toole, recognized the profound need to train church planters and pastors in nations with severely restricted Christian activity.

In May 1993, East-West was established to train and mentor faithful and reliable national pastors to become catalysts for indigenous church growth—reaching the lost with the gospel, equipping new believers, and multiplying reproducible churches.

Today, East-West works primarily in limited access countries and among unreached people groups in more than 60 countries worldwide so that disciples and churches will continuously multiply.

VISION
The vision of East-West is to glorify God by multiplying followers of Jesus in the spiritually darkest areas of the world.

MISSION
The mission of East-West is to mobilize the Body of Christ to evangelize the lost and equip local believers to multiply disciples and churches among the unreached.

GET INVOLVED

To learn more about East-West or to join the global ministry, visit www.eastwest.org/get-involved.

ABOUT ARISE

Arise is an initiative born out of East-West's desire to empower women around the world to be used by God to take the gospel to the nations. This is done by calling, connecting, and commissioning them to one another and to the heart and purposes of God in this hour.

There is a call from the Lord for women right now to live in the authority and identity given to them by Christ. We are connecting women to each other through stories and experiences. And women are being commissioned to be a powerful force for the kingdom of God.

That's why Arise exists.

We have hopeful expectation that as we call women to live boldly in the power of the Holy Spirit, connect them to each other for ongoing encouragement, and send them out on their unique mission, a culture of revival will break loose as families, communities, and nations are changed forever for the glory of God. Why? Because it's happened in the past.

Through women of our ancient past (such as Deborah, Ruth, Mary, and Lydia) and women of recent centuries (including Joan of Arc, Amy Carmichael, Corrie ten Boom, Mother Teresa, and Heidi Baker), God changed the world.

We believe that women who are moved by a passionate love for Jesus and who partner with Him to build His kingdom are a key to unlocking gospel movements in the world's spiritually dark places.

And now we are believing for 70 cities nationally and internationally to build this kingdom movement and mobilize women.

To learn more or to get involved with Arise, visit www.eastwest.org/arise.

NOTES

1   Murillo, Mario. *Vessels of Fire and Glory.* (Shippensburg, PA: Destiny Image Publishers, Inc., 2020) p. 42

2   Batterson, Mark. *The Circle Maker: Praying Circles Around Your Biggest Dreams and Greatest Fears.* (Grand Rapids, Michigan: Zondervan, 2016) p. 86

3   Murillo, Mario. *Vessels of Fire and Glory.* (Shippensburg, PA: Destiny Image Publishers, Inc., 2020) p. 145

4   Vawser, Lana. *The Prophetic Voice of God: Learning to Recognize the Language of the Holy Spirit.* (Shippensburg, PA: Destiny Image Publishers, Inc., 2018) p. 145

5   Murillo, Mario. *Vessels of Fire and Glory.* (Shippensburg, PA: Destiny Image Publishers, Inc., 2020) p. 42

6   Tozer, A. W. *Worship: The Reason We Were Created—Collected Insights from A. W. Tozer.* (Chicago, IL: Moody Publishers, 2017)

7   Alcorn, Randy. *The Treasure Principle: Unlocking the Secret of Joyful Giving.* (New York: Penguin Random House, LLC. 2005)

8   McCracken, Christina. *Live for That Day: Garnering Rewards at the Judgement Seat of Christ.* (Dallas, TX: His Publishing Group, 2019)

9   Vawser, Lana. *I Hear the Lord Say "New Era"*. (Shippensburg, PA: Destiny Image Publishers, Inc. 2020) p. 67

10 Bolz, Shawn. *Breakthrough: Prophecies, Prayers & Declarations*. (Studio City, CA: ICreate Productions, 2019) p. xvi

11 Johnson, Bill. *Hosting the Presence: Unveiling Heaven's Agenda*. (Shippensburg, PA: Destiny Image Publishers, Inc., 2012)

12 Vawser, Lana. *I Hear the Lord Say "New Era"*. (Shippensburg, PA: Destiny Image Publishers, Inc., 2020). p. 110

13 https://www.nationalgeographic.com/science/article/stars

14 https://www.sermonwriter.com/biblical-commentary/daniel-121-3/

15 https://lanavawser.com/2021/01/04/i-heard-the-lord-say-battle-weary-warriors-i-am-restoring-your-roar/

16 McCracken, Christina. *Live for that Day: Garnering Rewards at the Judgement Seat of Christ*. (Dallas, TX: His Publishing Group, 2019)

17 https://www.gardenguides.com/105993-root-system-oak-trees.html.

18 Vawser, Lana. *I Hear the Lord Say "New Era"*. (Shippensburg, PA: Destiny Image Publishers, Inc., 2020)

19 Wallnau, Lance. *God's Chaos Code: The Shocking Blueprint that Reveals 5 Keys to the Destiny of Nations*. (Keller, Texas: Killer Sheep Media, Inc., 2020)

20 King, Patricia and Sparks, Larry. *Arise: A Prophetic Call for Women to Receive Swords, Mantles and Kingdom Assignments*. (Shippensburg, PA: Destiny Image Publishers, Inc. 2018.) Baker, Heidi, p. 156

21 Lana Vawser. https://lanavawser.com/2020/11/19/prophets-of-go
d-under-intense-attack-i-hear-the-lord-say-stand-firm-you-will-not-be-t
aken-out-you-are-crossing-over-into-a-realm-of-carrying-my-wisdo
m-and-insight-like-never-before-my-voice-thro/

22 McClain-Walters, Michelle. *The Deborah Anointing: Embracing the
Call to be a Woman of Wisdom and Discernment.* (Lake Mary, Florida:
Charisma House, 2015) p. 2

23 Sheets, Dutch. https://www.givehim15.com/post/march-28-2021

24 King, Patricia and Sparks, Larry. *Arise: A Prophetic Call for Women to
Receive Swords, Mantles and Kingdom Assignments.* (Shippensburg, PA:
Destiny Image Publishers, Inc. 2018)

25 Murillo, Mario. *Vessels of Fire and Glory.* (Shippensburg, PA: Destiny
Image Publishers, Inc., 2020) p. 25

26 Vawser, Lana. https://lanavawser.com/2020/12/16/i-heard-the-lord-say
-daughters-of-god-receive-your-promise/

27 Viola, Frank. *From Eternity to Here: Rediscovering the Ageless Purpose of
God.* (Colorado Springs, CO: David C. Cook 2009). p. 128-129

28 Johnson, Bill. *Encountering the Goodness of God: 90 Daily Devotions.*
(Shippensburg, PA: Destiny Image Publishers, Inc. 2017)

29 Dawkins, Robby. *Do What Jesus Did.* (Bloomington, MN: Chosen
Books, 2013) p. 87

30 Heidi Baker. *Birthing the Miraculous.* (Lake Mary, FL: Charisma House,
2014) p. 46

WORKS CITED

Alcorn, Randy. *The Treasure Principle: Unlocking the Secret of Joyful Giving*. (New York: Penguin Random House, LLC. 2005)

Heidi Baker. *Birthing the Miraculous*. (Lake Mary, FL: Charisma House, 2014)

Batterson, Mark. *The Circle Maker: Praying Circles Around Your Biggest Dreams and Greatest Fears*. (Grand Rapids, Michigan: Zondervan, 2016)

Bolz, Shawn. *Breakthrough: Prophecies, Prayers & Declarations*. (Studio City, CA: ICreate Productions, 2019)

Dawkins, Robby. *Do What Jesus Did*. (Bloomington, MN: Chosen Books, 2013)

Johnson, Bill. *Hosting the Presence: Unveiling Heaven's Agenda*. (Shippensburg, PA: Destiny Image Publishers, Inc., 2012)

Johnson, Bill. *Encountering the Goodness of God: 90 Daily Devotions*. (Shippensburg, PA: Destiny Image Publishers, Inc. 2017)

King, Patricia and Sparks, Larry. *Arise: A Prophetic Call for Women to Receive Swords, Mantles and Kingdom Assignments*. (Shippensburg, PA: Destiny Image Publishers, Inc. 2018.) Baker, Heidi, p. 156

McClain-Walters, Michelle. *The Deborah Anointing: Embracing the Call to be a Woman of Wisdom and Discernment.* (Lake Mary, Florida: Charisma House, 2015)

McCracken, Christina. *Live for That Day: Garnering Rewards at the Judgement Seat of Christ.* (Dallas, TX: His Publishing Group, 2019)

Murillo, Mario. *Vessels of Fire and Glory.* (Shippensburg, PA: Destiny Image Publishers, Inc., 2020)

Sheets, Dutch. *Give Him 15.* https://www.givehim15.com/post/march-28-2021. Accessed May 21, 2021

Tozer, A. W. *Worship: The Reason We Were Created—Collected Insights from A. W. Tozer.* (Chicago, IL: Moody Publishers, 2017)

Vawser, Lana. *I Hear the Lord Say "New Era".* (Shippensburg, PA: Destiny Image Publishers, Inc. 2020)

Vawser, Lana. *The Prophetic Voice of God: Learning to Recognize the Language of the Holy Spirit.* (Shippensburg, PA: Destiny Image Publishers, Inc., 2018)

Vawser, Lana. https://www.lanavawser.com/2021/01/04/i-heard-the-lord-say-battle-weary-warriors-i-am-restoring-your-roar/. Accessed May 21, 2021

Vawser, Lana. https://www.lanavawser.com/2020/12/16/i-heard-the-lord-say-daughters-of-god-receive-your-promise/. Accessed May 21, 2021

Vawser, Lana. https://lanavawser.com/2020/11/19/prophets-of-god-under-intense-attack-i-hear-the-lord-say-stand-firm-you-will-not-be-taken-out-you-are-crossing-over-into-a-realm-of-carrying-my-wisdom-and-insight-like-never-before-my-voice-thro/. Accessed December 3, 2020

Viola, Frank. *From Eternity to Here: Rediscovering the Ageless Purpose of God.* (Colorado Springs, CO: David C. Cook, 2009)

Wallnau, Lance. *God's Chaos Code: The Shocking Blueprint that Reveals 5 Keys to the Destiny of Nations.* (Keller, Texas: Killer Sheep Media, Inc., 2020)

https://www.gardenguides.com/105993-root-system-oak-trees.html. Accessed March 3, 2021

https://www.nationalgeographic.com/science/article/stars. Accessed March 2, 2021

https://www.sermonwriter.com/biblical-commentary/daniel-121-3/. Accessed March 2, 2021

Made in the USA
Monee, IL
12 September 2021